A Year with Jesus

A Year with Jesus

Daily Readings and Meditations

Eugene H. Peterson

HarperSanFrancisco

A Division of HarperCollins*Publishers*

A YEAR WITH JESUS: *Daily Readings and Meditations.* Copyright © 2006 by Eugene H. Peterson. All rights reserved. Printed in the United States of America. No part of this book may be used or reproduced in any manner whatsoever without written permission except in the case of brief quotations embodied in critical articles and reviews. For information address HarperCollins Publishers, 10 East 53rd Street, New York, NY 10022.

HarperCollins books may be purchased for educational, business, or sales promotional use. For information please write: Special Markets Department, HarperCollins Publishers, 10 East 53rd Street, New York, NY 10022.

HarperCollins Web site: http://www.harpercollins.com

HarperCollins®, ® , and HarperSanFrancisco™ are trademarks of HarperCollins Publishers.

FIRST EDITION

Library of Congress Cataloging-in-Publication Data is available.
ISBN-10: 0-06-111843-5
ISBN-13: 978-0-06-111843-2

06 07 08 09 10 RRD(H) 10 9 8 7 6 5 4 3 2 1

For Lynn
In gratitude for gifts named and unnamed

A Year with Jesus

The goal of spending a year with Jesus is to learn how to pray. Our prayers do not start with us. They start with Jesus. Before we ever open our mouths in prayer, Jesus is praying for us. Despite much talk to the contrary, there are no secrets to living the Christian life. No prerequisite attitudes. No conditions more or less favorable to pursuing the Way. Anyone can do this, from any place, starting at any time. But it is only possible through prayer. We can only pray our lives into the way of following Jesus.

Prayer provides the primary language for everything that takes place in the way of Jesus. If we go to a shopping mall in North America, we speak English to get what we want. If we go to a restaurant in France, we speak French to order our meal. If we travel to Greece, we speak Greek to find our way to the Acropolis. And when we become personally involved with Jesus, we pray. We pray because it is the only language we have for speaking to the God revealed in Jesus. It is also the only language we have for listening to the commands and blessings and guidance that God provides in Jesus. God is nothing if not personal. Both God and we humans are most personal, most characteristically our unique selves, in our use of language. The language between God and us is called prayer.

What I want to insist on is that prayer is not something added on to the Christian life (or any life, for that matter). We cannot specialize in prayer any more than we can specialize in life. We cannot abstract prayer from our living, or isolate instances of prayer and study them under laboratory conditions. It is the language in which our lives are lived out, nurtured, developed, revealed, informed. The language in which we believe, love, explore, seek, and find. There are no shortcuts or detours: prayer is the cradle language among all those who are "born anew" and grow up to follow Jesus.

Prayer is a way of living. It is not a subject to be studied. It is not a technique to be learned. It is a life lived in response to God. We do not learn *about* prayer, we learn *to* pray; and the prayer, as it turns out, is never *just* prayer, but involves every dimension of our lives—eating, drinking, loving, working, walking, reading, singing. The way we follow Jesus must be internalized and embodied. That is what prayer does, gets Jesus inside us, gets his Spirit into our muscles and reflexes. There is no other way. Judas followed Jesus with his feet all over Palestine, but it never got inside him. Peter listened with his ears to everything Jesus said and spoke with his mouth the deepest truth about Jesus ("you are the Christ") but when he cut off the ear of Malchus in Gethsemane, we know that he hadn't learned that way of life from Jesus.

But because in our secularized society prayer is often associated with what people of "spiritual" interests pursue or with formal acts conducted by professional leaders, it is necessary from time to time to call attention to the fact that prayer is the street language that we use with Jesus as he walks the streets with us. We can't put off prayer until we "get good at it." It is the only language available to us as we bring our unique and particular selves, "just as we are without one plea," into daily, hourly conversation with God, who comes "just as he is" in Jesus.

Following Jesus necessarily means getting his words and ways into our everyday lives. It is not enough simply to recognize and approve his ways and get started in the right direction. Everything about Jesus is there to be embraced by our imaginations and assimilated into our habits—*believed* and *lived*. This takes place only as we *pray* while reading the story of Jesus, pray what we see Jesus doing, pray what we hear Jesus saying, pray the questions we have, pray the commands and promises and invitations that come to us in this story, pray the difficulties we encounter on the way.

Jesus's praying was never something apart from his living. We cannot isolate his praying from his living. His whole life is the context for understanding and then participating in his praying. It is the same with us: our entire lives provide circumstances and stuff for our prayers.

Jesus's life cannot be imposed from without. It cannot be copied. It must be shaped from within. This shaping takes place in prayer. The practice of prayer is the primary way by which the life of Jesus comes to permeate our entire lives so that we walk spontaneously and speak rhythmically in the fluidity and fluency of holiness. Left to ourselves we are fragmented and distracted people, jerky and spasmodic. Sin does that to us. The more object-like, the more thing-like, the more impersonal we become, the more disengaged we are from our God-created humanity and from the God-created world around us. Prayer, as the Spirit prays within us (and he most certainly does, whether we are aware of it or not— see Romans 8:19–26), recovers our original place in creation, so that we can live robustly in the world. Prayer in conversation with Jesus involves us firsthand in the grand reconciliation going on in Christ, setting us free for relational intimacies with family and friends, the heavens above us, and the earth under our feet (see Colossians 1:15–23). When we embrace the companionship of the praying Jesus, "Everything becomes a You and nothing remains an It" (paraphrasing W. H. Auden).

We pray with Jesus; Jesus prays with us. Day-by-day, week-by-week, month-by-month, Jesus—God with us—is prayed into the details of our lives, and God's salvation is formed in us.

In order to provide this text for prayer, your prayers and Jesus's prayers—a true conversation—I have taken the stories and words of Jesus from the Gospels of Saint Matthew and Saint John and spread them across a 365-day sequence of reading, reflection, and prayer. I interrupted Matthew two chapters from the end in order to let John provide the ending, and a most magnificent ending it is. My intent is that your reading of Jesus turns into praying with Jesus, keeping His delightful company as lover and friend.

January 1

The Book of the Genealogy

An account of the genealogy of Jesus the Messiah, the son of David, the son of Abraham.

Matthew 1:1

Three names mark key points in God's salvation work: Abraham, father of the faithful; David, the man after God's own heart; Jesus, the son of God, who summed up Abraham and David and revealed all that God is for us.

Why are ancestors important?

You come, Jesus, out of a history thick with names. Names—not dates, not events—signal the junctures in which you single out myself and others for personal love and responsibility. Named, I now name your name in trust and gratefulness: Jesus. Amen.

Of Whom Jesus Was Born

Abraham was the father of Isaac, and Isaac the father of Jacob, and Jacob the father of Judah and his brothers and Judah the father of Perez and Zerah by Tamar, and Perez the father of Hezron, and Hezron the father of Aram and Aram the father of Aminadab, and Aminadab the father of Nahshon, . . . and Eliud the father of Eleazar, and Eleazar the father of Matthan, and Matthan the father of Jacob and Jacob the father of Joseph the husband of Mary, of whom Jesus was born, who is called the Messiah. So all the generations from Abraham to David are fourteen generations; and from David to the deportation to Babylon, fourteen generations; and from the deportation to Babylon to the Messiah, fourteen generations.

MATTHEW 1:2–17

The biblical fondness for genealogical lists is not dull obscurantism, it is an insistence on the primacy and continuity of people. Each name is a burnished link connecting God's promises to his fulfillments in the chain of people who are the story of God's mercy. Which of these names stands out for you?

Some of these names I don't recognize at all, God. And that is reassuring! I don't have to be an Abraham or a David to be included in this salvation litany. My ordinariness is as essential as another's extraordinariness. Thank you. Amen.

By Tamar

And Judah the father of Perez and Zerah by Tamar, and Perez the father of Hezron, and Hezron the father of Aram ... and Salmon the father of Boaz by Rahab, and Boaz the father of Obed by Ruth, and Obed the father of Jesse and Jesse the father of King David. And David was the father of Solomon by the wife of Uriah.

MATTHEW 1:3,5–6

Four names in the list are a surprise: Tamar, Rahab, Ruth, and the wife of Uriah (Bathsheba). Each of these names represents a person who was exploited, or downtrodden, or an outsider—the misused, the immoral, the foreign. Jesus's genealogy doesn't prove racial or moral purity, but redemptive range. God's salvation work is inclusive, not exclusive.

What do you know of each of these women?

Do I have enough confidence, Lord, in your inventive and incorporative will, to believe that you will use unattractive, immoral, and unlovely people as well as the glamorous and virtuous and admirable? That is hard to believe, but the evidence is impressive. Help my unbelief. Amen.

All the Generations

And Jacob the father of Joseph the husband of Mary, of whom Jesus was born, who is called the Messiah. So all the generations from Abraham to David are fourteen generations; and from David to the deportation to Babylon, fourteen generations; and from the deportation to Babylon to the Messiah, fourteen generations.

MATTHEW 1:16–17

The list concludes with a name (Jesus) plus a title (Messiah). The forty-two generations conclude with Jesus, who is given the title Christ (in Hebrew, Messiah), the person whom God anoints to accomplish our salvation. The final name is simultaneously a human life and a divine work.

What does the name Jesus Christ mean to you?

I see, Father, that you do not simply permit names to accumulate at random, but that you shape lives. There is a design and there is a goal. Enter my earth-conditioned existence and shape eternity in me. Amen.

January 5

The Birth of Jesus the Messiah

Now the birth of Jesus the Messiah took place in this way. When his mother Mary had been engaged to Joseph, but before they lived together, she was found to be with child from the Holy Spirit.

MATTHEW 1:18

There is a combination of old and new in this birth story: traditional angels, visions, prophecies; there is also the miraculously innovative divine spirit. There are historical data; there is also virginal conception.

Why is the virgin birth significant?

I am not satisfied with reading about your birth, Lord, I want to be in on it. Take the ancient history of my childhood and religion and put it to use. Make the birth of Christ as vivid and actual in me as it was in Mary. Amen.

Joseph, Being a Righteous Man

Her husband Joseph, being a righteous man and unwilling to expose her to public disgrace, planned to dismiss her quietly. But just when he had resolved to do this, an angel of the Lord appeared to him in a dream and said, "Joseph, son of David, do not be afraid to take Mary as your wife, for the child conceived in her is from the Holy Spirit."

MATTHEW 1:19–20

Joseph thought that "righteous" involved doing the proper thing; he is about to find out that it is also being the right person. The word "righteous" changes meaning in this event, a change from loyalty to a moral tradition to obedience to a divine person. Faith crowds out duty and wisdom as the dynamic of the "righteous man."

How would you describe the "righteous person"?

Father, with my flat-earth ideas of "righteous," there is no way I can respond appropriately to your presence unless you break into my imagination "in a dream." I will pray expectantly, open to your vision. How else will I receive guidance for becoming a righteous person? Amen.

Name Him Jesus

"She will bear a son, and you are to name him Jesus, for he will save his people from their sins." All this took place to fulfill what had been spoken by the Lord through the prophet:

MATTHEW 1:21–22

Mary's work is giving birth; Joseph's work is naming. Much attention has been given, appropriately enough, to Mary. But why the avoidance of Joseph? He was set apart for the priestly-poetic task of naming a character and defing a destiny.

What does the name Jesus mean?

Jesus, your name defines the gospel: not a model that I can admire and follow, but a Savior entering the world of my troubled heart and doing something, saving me. Amen.

January 8

Spoken ... Through the Prophet

All this took place to fulfill what had been spoken by the Lord through the prophet: "Look, the virgin shall conceive and bear a son, and they shall name him Emmanuel," which means, "God is with us."

MATTHEW 1:22–23

A deep, contrapuntal resonance reverberates between Isaiah's prophecy and Mary's pregnancy. Half-formed expectations take shape embryonically. Obscurely imagined messianic hopes get a character and a name.

Read and compare Isaiah 7:1–14.

There are promises and longings out of my past, my infancy and childhood, O God, that you fulfill in the birth of Jesus in my life. Complete the fulfillment, being with me in your fullness. Amen.

January 9

He Did . . .

When Joseph awoke from sleep, he did as the angel of the Lord commanded him; he took her as his wife but had no marital relations with her until she had borne a son; and he named him Jesus.

MATTHEW 1:24–25

It is one thing to have dreams, another thing to act on them. Joseph both dreamed and acted—a perfect model of obedience. He affirmed the action of the Holy Spirit in his closest personal relationship, he refrained from interfering in the divine process, and he did what he was told.

Why is Joseph important in your life?

When I observe the action of this mature, free man, Lord—the reckless involvement, the disciplined restraint, the plain obedience, and all of it woven together in one coherent righteous action—I know that I, too, can live in daring obedience before you. Amen.

January 10

Jesus/Herod

In the time of King Herod, after Jesus was born in Bethlehem of Judea, wise men from the East came to Jerusalem,

MATTHEW 2:1

The two names, Jesus and Herod, are in contrast. The general ("in the time of Herod") gives way to the particular ("Jesus was born"). Kingship comes into focus. Rule is personalized. Geography and politics slip into mere background as Jesus centers all history.

What are you most interested in?

God, when I see how kings and nations slip into the shadows at Jesus's birth, I see that I will do well not to become engrossed in either of them. It will not be by excavating Bethlehem or by analyzing Herod, but by worshiping you that my life will find center and purpose. Amen.

January 11

Wise Men

In the time of King Herod, after Jesus was born in Bethlehem of Judea, wise men from the East came to Jerusalem, asking, "Where is the child who has been born king of the Jews? For we observed his star at its rising, and have come to pay him homage.

MATTHEW 2:1–2

The wise men were experts in the movement of the stars and signs in the heavens. Their inquiry thrusts the provincial village into a cosmic concern. It is not scientific data they are searching out, but a person to worship. True wisdom is not gathering information; it is adoration of God's revealed truth.

What is your favorite story of the wise men?

Teach me this wisdom, Lord: I often treat worship as a means to some other end, intellectual or material. But the wise men didn't come to the Christ as scholars to learn more, or as wealthy tycoons to amass more plunder; they came to worship. Amen.

January 12

He Was Frightened

When King Herod heard this, he was frightened, and all Jerusalem with him; and calling together all the chief priests and scribes of the people, he inquired of them where the Messiah was to be born. They told him, "In Bethlehem of Judea; for so it has been written by the prophet . . ."

Matthew 2:3–5

While the magi approached the birth of Jesus with reverential awe, Herod, hearing the news, was full of dread. It is possible to fashion values and goals so defiant of God that any rumor of his reality shakes our foundation.

What are your values?

Prevent, O God, the Herodian spirit from filtering into my life: the spirit that uses religion to protect itself, and jealous of any hint of rivalry, responds to your Spirit only with suspicious fear. Amen.

January 13

By No Means Least

They told him, "In Bethlehem of Judea; for so it has been written by the prophet: 'And you, Bethlehem, in the land of Judah, are by no means least among the rulers of Judah; for from you shall come a ruler who is to shepherd my people Israel.'"

MATTHEW 2:5–6

Even obscure items of geography—little Bethlehem, for instance—by prophetic designation play their part in the messianic history. The village is now one of the best known on earth. Significance comes not from size but from the Savior.

Where is Bethlehem?

"O holy Child of Bethlehem, descend to us, we pray; cast out our sin, and enter in, be born in us today. We hear the Christmas angels the great glad tidings tell; O come to us, abide with us, our Lord Emmanuel." * Amen.

---

* Phillips Brooks, "O Little Town of Bethlehem," *The Hymnbook* (Presbyterian Church in the United States, United Presbyterian Church in the U.S.A., and Reformed Church in America: 1955), 157.

Search Diligently

Then Herod secretly called for the wise men and learned from them the exact time when the star had appeared. Then he sent them to Bethlehem, saying, "Go and search diligently for the child; and when you have found him, bring me word so that I may also go and pay him homage."

MATTHEW 2:7–8

Herod, impressive and fearful to his contemporaries, looks merely ridiculous to us. His secret, lying intrigues are useless before the ingenuous, unarmed invasion of history in Jesus at Bethlehem.

Who, to you, is the most impressive person in current history?

I am so used to being intimidated by conspiratorial evil, God, that I lose touch with the reality that your will is done, that your kingdom comes, and that the rulers of this world have very little to say about it, one way or the other. All praise to your omnipotent grace, your eternal love. Amen.

Where the Child Was

When they had heard the king, they set out; and there, ahead of them, went the star that they had seen at its rising, until it stopped over the place where the child was. When they saw that the star had stopped, they were overwhelmed with joy.

MATTHEW 2:9–10

The dogma of the astrologer is that stars are impersonal cosmic arrangements that determine personal fate; the gospel is that stars are in God's services "for signs" (Genesis 1:14). This star signals not our fate, but our freedom.

Why were the magi glad?

"When I look at thy heavens, the work of thy fingers, the moon and the stars which thou has established; what is man that thou art mindful of him, and the son of man that thou dost care for him?" (Psalm 8:3–4). Amen.

They Knelt Down and Paid Him Homage

On entering the house, they saw the child with Mary his mother; and they knelt down and paid him homage. Then, opening their treasure chests, they offered him gifts of gold, frankincense, and myrrh.

MATTHEW 2:11

The first thing that wise people do in the presence of Jesus is worship: not congratulate themselves on having found him, not ask him questions, not attempt to get something from him, but offer up themselves to him.

How do you worship?

In your presence, Lord Jesus, I want my life to be changed from getting things, to giving myself, so that I may grow into wholeness. Amen.

January 17

Warned in a Dream

And having been warned in a dream not to return to Herod, they left for their own country by another road.

Matthew 2:12

A meeting with Herod would have been highly dramatic, just the kind of encounter that journalists delight in covering. Yet there is to be no dissipation of the act of worship in satisfying a king's curiosity, but an immediate return to everyday living in "their own country."

What are some results of worship?

God, connect the deepening and centering of life that I experience in moments of worship with the routines and duties of my weekday hours so that all of life will be glorified by your presence. Amen.

January 18

Flee to Egypt

Now after they had left, an angel of the Lord appeared to Joseph in a dream and said, "Get up, take the child and his mother, and flee to Egypt, and remain there until I tell you; for Herod is about to search for the child, to destroy him." Then Joseph got up, took the child and his mother by night, and went to Egypt and remained there until the death of Herod. This was to fulfill what had been spoken by the Lord through the prophet, "Out of Egypt I have called my son."

MATTHEW 2:13–15

Herod's threat, which seems so ominous, is scarcely more than a pretext for accomplishing God's will. The flight into Egypt, retracing the ancient route of redemption, is part of a finely wrought salvation history.

What associations does Egypt have for you?

Lord, I see that Herod is real enough: he opens scenes, he triggers sequences, but he doesn't cause anything. Evil can't. Only you, God, cause, and what you cause is salvation, through Jesus, my Lord and Savior. Amen.

Rachel Weeping

When Herod saw that he had been tricked by the wise men, he was infuriated, and he sent and killed all the children in and around Bethlehem who were two years old or under, according to the time that he had learned from the wise men. Then was fulfilled what had been spoken through the prophet Jeremiah: "A voice was heard in Ramah, wailing and loud lAmentation, Rachel weeping for her children; she refused to be consoled, because they are no more."

MATTHEW 2:16–18

The slaughtered children participate in the messianic birth pangs: Christ enters a world flailing in rebellion. Herod, in a tantrum, hysterically tries to hold on to his kingdom. The voice in Ramah reverberates in history's echo chambers and gets louder every year.

What is the worst crime you are aware of?

Dear God, so much weeping! Such a burden of lamentation! I will not gloss over the terrible pain and sorrow that comes from vanity and anger, but neither will I forget the final word of resurrection. Amen.

Herod Died

When Herod died, an angel of the Lord suddenly appeared in a dream to Joseph in Egypt and said, "Get up, take the child and his mother, and go to the land of Israel, for those who were seeking the child's life are dead." Then Joseph got up, took the child and his mother, and went to the land of Israel. But when he heard that Archelaus was ruling over Judea in place of his father Herod, he was afraid to go there. And after being warned in a dream, he went away to the district of Galilee. There he made his home in a town called Nazareth, so that what had been spoken through the prophets might be fulfilled, "He will be called a Nazorean."

MATTHEW 2:19–23

Jesus's life begins with men seeking to kill him; it ends in a similar atmosphere of conspiracy and violence. But the violence and plotting are as ineffective at the beginning as at the end. The holy family enters the holy land. Salvation gathers to full expression in a nuclear family in a provincial land.

How many dreams has Joseph had?

I trace out of my memory, O God, stories that have been fashioned on this old road between Egypt and Israel: stories of Abraham, and of Joseph and Moses; stories of faith and blessing and salvation. Thank you for including me in the stories. Amen.

January 21

In the Wilderness ... Proclaiming

In those days John the Baptist appeared in the wilderness of Judea, proclaiming, "Repent, for the kingdom of heaven has come near." This is the one of whom the prophet Isaiah spoke when he said, "The voice of one crying out in the wilderness: 'Prepare the way of the Lord, make his paths straight.'"

MATTHEW 3:1–3

The ancient Judean desert is the site of John's Messiah-readiness preaching. Everything is stark in the desert: the life-and-death contrasts, the vividness of minute details, the absence of the superfluous, the emptiness. "Shall we never permit our hands to be empty so we may grasp what only empty hands can grasp?"*

What does "at hand" mean?

In this moment of silence and emptiness, O God, I wait and listen. Purge my spirit of sloth and train it in alert, messianic expectation. "In the deserts of the heart let the healing fountains start."† Amen.

---

* Karl Barth, *Epistle to the Romans* (London: Oxford University Press, 1933), 380.

† W. H. Auden, "In Memory of W. B. Yeats," *Collected Poems,* Edward Mendelson, ed. (New York: Random House, 1976), 198.

John

Now John wore clothing of camel's hair with a leather belt around his waist, and his food was locusts and wild honey. Then the people of Jerusalem and all Judea were going out to him, and all the region along the Jordan and they were baptized by him in the river Jordan, confessing their sins.

MATTHEW 3:4–6

John's food and clothing defy fashion. He finds his identity not among market-oriented contemporaries, but among God-oriented prophets. John's single-mindedness proceeds from a deep immersion in the prophetic imagination and spirit.

Compare John with Elijah the Tishbite (2 Kings 1:8).

Lord, are there ways in which I can take the daily necessities of food and clothing and use them to complement and reinforce my relation with you? I will begin by giving thanks for them, in the name of Jesus Christ. Amen.

January 23

Who Warned You to Flee?

But when he saw many Pharisees and Sadducees coming for baptism, he said to them, "You brood of vipers! Who warned you to flee from the wrath to come? Bear fruit worthy of repentance. Do not presume to say to yourselves, 'We have Abraham as our ancestor'; for I tell you, God is able from these stones to raise up children to Abraham. Even now the ax is lying at the root of the trees; every tree therefore that does not bear good fruit is cut down and thrown into the fire."

MATTHEW 3:7–10

Fleeing from wrath is not a gospel. The base lives and cowardly souls of the "brood of vipers" are rushing to the Jordan for rescue. But John will not indulge their escapism; he calls them to responsible action: "bear fruit worthy of repentance!"

What does repentance mean?

I am more comfortable, Father, with an image of you as a gentleman farmer, pruning an occasional branch and raking up a few leaves. But you go to the root. I submit myself to your surgery, and hope in your salvation. Amen.

January 24

He Will Baptize You

"I baptize you with water for repentance, but one who is more powerful than I is coming after me; I am not worthy to carry his sandals. He will baptize you with the Holy Spirit and fire. His winnowing fork is in his hand, and he will clear his threshing floor and will gather his wheat into the granary; but the chaff he will burn with unquenchable fire."

MATTHEW 3:11–12

Two aspects of Jesus's baptism are described under the images of wind and fire. The wind brings something to us (the very breath of God), the fire takes something away from us (the worthless chaff of our sins). Threshing is not always pleasant business, especially when we are the grain. But the results are good. Who wants to be mixed with chaff forever?

Contrast the two baptisms.

I am grateful, God, that you take me with such seriousness and labor over me with such care. I see myself now thrown into the air by your threshing shovel, sifted and cleansed by the wind of your Spirit, ready for use in your granaries. Amen.

January 25

Baptized

Then Jesus came from Galilee to John at the Jordan, to be baptized by him. John would have prevented him, saying, "I need to be baptized by you, and do you come to me?" But Jesus answered him, "Let it be so now; for it is proper for us in this way to fulfill all righteousness." Then he consented. And when Jesus had been baptized, just as he came up from the water, suddenly the heavens were opened to him and he saw the Spirit of God descending like a dove and alighting on him. And a voice from heaven said, "This is my Son, the Beloved, with whom I am well pleased."

MATTHEW 3:13–17

Baptism personalizes the primordial Genesis beginnings. Just as the Spirit brooded birdlike over the ancient ocean deeps, so the Spirit "descending like a dove" is poised over the baptismal waters. The "it is good" of creation is completed by the "well-pleased" in Christ.

What does your baptism mean?

I praise you, Almighty God, for speaking creative and eternity-shaping words over me, for showing me the goodness of your creation, and blessing me with the peace of your acceptance in Christ. Amen.

He Fasted Forty Days

Then Jesus was led up by the Spirit into the wilderness to be tempted by the devil. He fasted forty days and forty nights, and afterwards he was famished.

MATTHEW 4:1–2

Moses was forty days on the mountain, in preparation for God's revelation; Elijah was forty days in the desert, in preparation for God's still small voice; Jesus is forty days in the wilderness, prepared for the testing that will qualify him for the work of salvation.

What is the purpose of fasting?

What testing will you lead me into today, Lord? Prepare my heart so that I hear your word, and am led by your Spirit. Show me how to meet each test with energy and faith, trusting your victory in Christ. Amen.

January 27

Loaves of Bread

The tempter came and said to him, 'If you are the Son of God, command these stones to become loaves of bread.' But he answered, "It is written, 'One does not live by bread alone, but by every word that comes from the mouth of God.'"

MATTHEW 4:3-4

Bread, necessary though it is, is not primary: God is primary. Jesus will let nothing, not even necessary things, interfere with that primacy. Jesus will not use God to get what he wants; he submits himself to being what God wants.

How do you face this temptation?

Not what I want, but what you want, O God. Guard me from all temptations to use you to satisfy my appetites. What I want mostly is to acquire new appetites, a hunger for righteousness, that will be satisfied by your word. Amen.

January 28

The Pinnacle of the Temple

Then the devil took him to the holy city and placed him on the pinnacle of the temple saying to him, "If you are the Son of God, throw yourself down; for it is written, 'He will command his angels concerning you,' and 'On their hands they will bear you up, so that you will not dash your foot against a stone.'" Jesus said to him, "Again it is written, 'Do not put the Lord your God to the test.'"

MATTHEW 4:5–7

Miracles, attractive as they are, are not primary: God is primary. Jesus will not engage in a miracle-making that dazzles and entertains. Jesus will not use God as a means of showing off, or attracting admirers. He has far more important things to do, working love and salvation.

How do you face this temptation?

Lord, protect me from being distracted by the sensational, from being diverted by the extraordinary. Keep me faithful in the daily round, attending to the common details of mercy and holiness. Amen.

January 29

A Very High Mountain

Again, the devil took him to a very high mountain and showed him all the kingdoms of the world and their splendor; and he said to him, "All these I will give you, if you will fall down and worship me." Jesus said to him, "Away with you, Satan! for it is written, 'Worship the Lord your God, and serve only him.'"

MATTHEW 4:8–10

Power, important as it is, is not primary: God is primary. Jesus will not negotiate for power, even though he would be able to use the power benevolently. Goodness must not be compelled; love may not be coerced. The kingdom will come into being "not by might nor by power, but by Thy Spirit."

How do you face this temptation?

Lord, how often I face this temptation, the temptation to make people be good, to force them into the ways of righteousness. I always know so well what is good for others! Forgive me, Father, and give me the quiet, determined patience to love in mercy, to wait in hope. Amen.

January 30

Jesus Began to Proclaim

Then the devil left him, and suddenly angels came and waited on him. Now when Jesus heard that John had been arrested, he withdrew to Galilee. He left Nazareth and made his home in Capernaum by the sea, in the territory of Zebulun and Naphtali, so that what had been spoken through the prophet Isaiah might be fulfilled: "Land of Zebulun, land of Naphtali, on the road by the sea, across the Jordan, Galilee of the Gentiles—the people who sat in darkness have seen a great light, and for those who sat in the region and shadow of death light has dawned." From that time Jesus began to proclaim, "Repent, for the kingdom of heaven has come near.

MATTHEW 4:11–17

Thoroughly prepared by the temptations, Jesus begins his ministry. Isaiah provides the text, Capernaum the pulpit. The message calls everyone to alert response: God is at hand doing the work of making his will a present reality in salvation.

Compare Jesus's sermon with John the Baptist's.

What power, God, in these words! What life-changing truth, what mercy-releasing grace. I live in your presence, not the hope of your presence; I participate in what is happening even now, not in what I wish would happen. Amen.

As He Walked by the Sea

As he walked by the Sea of Galilee, he saw two brothers, Simon, who is called Peter, and Andrew his brother, casting a net into the sea—for they were fishermen. And he said to them, "Follow me, and I will make you fish for people." Immediately they left their nets and followed him. As he went from there, he saw two other brothers, James son of Zebedee and his brother John, in the boat with their father Zebedee, mending their nets, and he called them. Immediately they left the boat and their father, and followed him.

MATTHEW 4:18–22

Jesus begins his work along the Galilean Sea, not at the Jerusalem Temple. The world of common work, not the world of religious ritual, is where discipleship starts. And fishermen, not priests, are the first disciples. Jesus comes to us, where we are, and initiates the work of kingdom-making.

What does Jesus call you from?

As you speak your commands to me, O Christ, complete your will in me. Convert me from a way of life bound to things to a life related to persons. The nets have absorbed my attention long enough; lead me into your way of being human. Amen.

Up the Mountain

When Jesus saw the crowds, he went up the mountain; and after he sat down, his disciples came to him. Then he began to speak, and taught them, saying:

MATTHEW 5:1–2

Surrounded by new disciples, Jesus begins the teaching that will train them in the new life, which is God's kingdom. No words rival these in importance or power.

What do you know about the Sermon on the Mount?

My hope, Lord, as I attend to your teaching, is that I will be formed into your likeness, not just informed about what you once spoke to your disciples. I want to be thoroughly taught by you so that I can thoroughly live for you. Amen.

February 2

The Poor in Spirit

"Blessed are the poor in spirit, for theirs is the kingdom of heaven."

MATTHEW 5:3

Self-made and self-sufficient people live in a fantasy world, empty of the reality of God. In contrast, the poor in spirit are deeply aware of being God-made and God-sufficient: everything derives from the goodness of God and everything depends on the grace of God.

What does poor in spirit mean to you?

I empty my life, God, of all god-substitutes and all idol-alternatives. I have nothing, so that I can receive everything. A life rich in wonder and blessing. Amen.

February 3

Those Who Mourn

"Blessed are those who mourn, for they will be comforted."

MATTHEW 5:4

The willingness to respond to pain, to misfortune, to suffering, enables us to participate in the divine compassion that changes damnation to redemption. Sorrow does not get stuck in despair, but discovers comfort.

Whose sorrow do you share?

"O come and mourn with me a while; O come ye to the Savior's side; O come, together let us mourn: Jesus, our Lord, is crucified! A broken heart, a fount of tears, ask, and they will not be denied; a broken heart love's cradle is: Jesus, our Lord, is crucified!" * Amen.

---

* F. W. Faber, "O Come and Mourn with Me a While," *The Hymnbook*, 174.

February 4

The Meek

"Blessed are the meek, for they will inherit the earth."

MATTHEW 5:5

In a day when assertiveness is in vogue, meekness is likely to be dismissed out of hand. A precise understanding helps: it is not slack laziness, but disciplined ambition; in place of riotous aggression, controlled obedience.

Who is the meekest person you know?

Lord Jesus Christ, I will not deny my vitality or squelch my energy, but I will place them under your rule so that they will serve your purposes. I will not harness you to my requirements, but offer myself to yours. Amen.

February 5

Hunger and Thirst

"Blessed are those who hunger and thirst for righteousness, for they will be filled."

MATTHEW 5:6

Righteousness is food and drink for the whole person. It is never listed among the basic dietary items in the nutrition textbooks, but it is more important than any of them.

How do you express your appetite for righteousness?

I hunger and thirst after your righteousness, dear God: feed me on the bread of heaven, quench my thirst with the cup of blessing. Daily I will dine at your table, with Jesus as my host. Amen.

February 6

The Merciful

"Blessed are the merciful, for they will receive mercy."

MATTHEW 5:7

God responds to our misfortunes, our ignorances, our failures, and our disobediences in ways that draw us close to him and save us from our trouble. Mercy. It is the opposite of the harsh condemnation, which rejects. Because God does it, we can do it.

Who has treated you with unexpected mercy?

God, even as I have been accepted by you in mercy, help me to accept others—not condemning, not rejecting, not scolding, but sharing the promises of salvation through the mercies of Jesus Christ. Amen.

The Pure in Heart

"Blessed are the pure in heart, for they will see God."

MATTHEW 5:8

Dilettantes shop for God as they would for a new pair of shoes. Their purposes vacillate and they live distracted. But simple intention is the way to comprehension and fellowship. "Purity of heart is to will one thing."*

What distracts you from God?

I have a difficult time, God, silencing the competing voices, shutting out the seductive images. I want you, but I want a lot of other things, too. "Unite my heart to fear thy name" (Psalm 86:11). Amen.

* Soren Kierkegaard, *Purity of Heart* (New York: Harper & Row, 1956), 53.

February 8

The Peacemakers

"Blessed are the peacemakers, for they will be called children of God."

MATTHEW 5:9

Life in God's kingdom is not a competitive survival of the fittest. The prize does not go to the strongest and the swiftest. Jesus teaches us how to make peace with our neighbors, evoking the best in them, not destroy them as dangerous rivals.

Are you better at competition or cooperation?

Show me how to use my life, Jesus, in ways that will make others better, not get the better of them. I will no longer look at others as competitors for your favor, but as companions in your life of peacemaking. Amen.

February 9

Persecuted

"Blessed are those who are persecuted for righteousness' sake, for theirs is the kingdom of heaven."

MATTHEW 5:10

Lest we think that the peacemakers of verse 9 are bland, gray-flannel conformists who are afraid to rock the boat, Jesus defines our righteousness as that which frequently provokes opposition in a world whose values are called into question.

Who doesn't approve of your life in Christ?

When the storms of opposition come, dear Christ, keep me "steadfast, immovable, always abounding in the work of the Lord." Root me in righteousness so that my growth is impervious to popular dissent, and always faithful to you. Amen.

Rejoice and Be Glad

"Blessed are you when people revile you and persecute you and utter all kinds of evil against you falsely on my account. Rejoice and be glad, for your reward is great in heaven, for in the same way they persecuted the prophets who were before you."

MATTHEW 5:11–12

If we take the offensive against our opposition, we are liable to harshness and bluster; if we get on the defensive, we lose initiative and appear timid and unsure: When we dance our faith, the enemy is disarmed and drawn into the celebration. Leaping joy is the sanity of blessing in a lunatic society.

What do you have cause to rejoice in?

Lord God, I will not use the world's weapons to fight your battles; and I will not be backed into a corner by those who scorn your love. Be with me as I celebrate my witness in joy, and announce my confidence with gladness, for Jesus's sake. Amen.

Salt

"You are the salt of the earth; but if salt has lost its taste, how can its saltiness be restored? It is no longer good for anything, but is thrown out and trampled under foot."

MATTHEW 5:13

Minuscule and insignificant as each individual Christian is, yet we are God's way of preserving society, of sharpening the taste buds of civilization. Our usefulness is not in what we do, but in what we are by God's grace.

What are the main uses of salt in your life?

Father, I keep thinking I have to rush out and do something; you keep calling me back to be someone. Use this life that you have created and redeemed to preserve and enhance those among whom I live today. Amen.

February 12

Light

"You are the light of the world. A city built on a hill cannot be hid. No one after lighting a lamp puts it under the bushel basket, but on the lampstand, and it gives light to all in the house."

MATTHEW 5:14–15

Salt is a powerful, hidden influence; light is a blazing public illumination. Christian disciples are not only a behind-the-scenes influence, but also an out-in-the-open enlightenment.

What are the main uses of light in your life?

You, Lord, the light of the world, be light in me so that my life shows the clarity and warmth of your salvation. I would not darken anyone's path by the shadows of my doubts or the gloom of my unbelief. Amen.

February 13

Good Works

"In the same way, let your light shine before others, so that they may see your good works and give glory to your Father in heaven."

MATTHEW 5:16

Good works are an important means of witness; but they are also extremely susceptible to pride. Jesus can teach us how to use good works as glorifications of God, and not simply as advertisements of ourselves.

What are some of your good works?

"So let our lips and lives express the holy gospel we profess; so let our works and virtues shine, to prove the doctrine all divine. Thus shall we best proclaim abroad the honors of our Savior God, when His salvation reigns within, and grace subdues the power of sin." Amen.

* Isaac Watts, "So Let Our Lips and Lives Express," *The Hymnbook*, 250.

February 14

Fulfill

"Do not think that I have come to abolish the law or the prophets; I have come not to abolish but to fulfill. For truly I tell you, until heaven and earth pass away, not one letter, not one stroke of a letter, will pass from the law until all is accomplished. Therefore, whoever breaks one of the least of these commandments, and teaches others to do the same, will be called least in the kingdom of heaven; but whoever does them and teaches them will be called great in the kingdom of heaven. For I tell you, unless your righteousness exceeds that of the scribes and Pharisees, you will never enter the kingdom of heaven."

MATTHEW 5:17–20

No detail in the law and the prophets was corrupt or obsolete. But much of it was empty. Sin cracks had appeared and the vitality had leaked out. But Jesus does not therefore discard them—fulfill is the gospel program.

How does Jesus fulfill the law and the prophets?

I see, Father, that there is nothing that you once used that cannot be used again. Lead me into the eternal meanings of your ancient words so that I may live in a present obedience, Christ living in me. Amen.

February 15

Exceeds

"For I tell you, unless your righteousness exceeds that of the scribes and Pharisees, you will never enter the kingdom of heaven."

MATTHEW 5:20

Religion that is a matter of careful, moral calculation is all wrong. The gospel requires a leap of faith. Christ does not counsel a safe, manageable morality that anyone can learn in ten easy lessons, but a reckless adventurous life commitment.

What was the righteousness of the scribes?

I do not want to be a religious bookkeeper, Lord, but a faith explorer, ready to take risks without counting the cost, ready to love without taking out insurance against suffering, ready to plunge into obedience without calculating my rewards. Amen.

February 16

If You Are Angry

"You have heard that it was said to those of ancient times, 'You shall not murder'; and 'whoever murders shall be liable to judgment.' But I say to you that if you are angry with a brother or sister, you will be liable to judgment; and if you insult a brother or sister, you will be liable to the council; and if you say, 'You fool,' you will be liable to the hell of fire. So when you are offering your gift at the altar, if you remember that your brother or sister has something against you, leave your gift there before the altar and go; first be reconciled to your brother or sister, and then come and offer your gift. Come to terms quickly with your accuser while you are on the way to court with him, or your accuser may hand you over to the judge, and the judge to the guard, and you will be thrown into prison. Truly I tell you, you will never get out until you have paid the last penny."

MATTHEW 5:21–26

The old commandment was intended to protect relationships, not just prevent murders. Anger that treats another contemptuously is murderous. Feelings that divide persons are destructive. Obedience reduced to only not doing something is half-obedience.

Why is anger dangerous?

Do I diminish others, reduce them, despise them, God? With your help and direction I will augment them, respect them, and exalt them. Amen.

Tear It Out

"You have heard that it was said, 'You shall not commit adultery.' But I say to you that everyone who looks at a woman with lust has already committed adultery with her in his heart. If your right eye causes you to sin, tear it out and throw it away; it is better for you to lose one of your members than for your whole body to be thrown into hell. And if your right hand causes you to sin, cut it off and throw it away; it is better for you to lose one of your members than for your whole body to go into hell."

MATTHEW 5:27–30

No spirit surgery is too costly and no self-discipline too exacting in our development as Christ's servants. Our sin-split personalities think one thing and do another, or do one thing and think another. Jesus trains us in a mastery over self that brings us into single-minded devotion.

Compare this with 2 Corinthians 10:3–6.

Help me, O Christ, to maintain a ruthless mastery over my pride and self-centeredness so that every part of my life may be coordinated in acts of love. Amen.

Divorce

"It was also said, 'Whoever divorces his wife, let him give her a certificate of divorce.' But I say to you that anyone who divorces his wife,
except on the ground of unchastity, causes her to commit adultery;
and whoever marries a divorced woman commits adultery."

MATTHEW 5:31–32

The guardian commandment on love, designed to protect intimate personal relationships, in practice had become the occasion
for casuistic legalism. Jesus returns our attention to people and
what happens to them.

What is wrong with divorce?

*God, I know that you give commandments as tools that will express your
love, share your grace, and communicate your will, not as formulas for
making me righteous. Help me to use them your way. For Jesus's sake.
Amen.*

Do Not Swear at All

"Again, you have heard that it was said to those of ancient times, 'You shall not swear falsely, but carry out the vows you have made to the Lord.' But I say to you, Do not swear at all, either by heaven, for it is the throne of God, or by the earth, for it is his footstool, or by Jerusalem, for it is the city of the great King. And do not swear by your head, for you cannot make one hair white or black. Let your word be 'Yes, Yes' or 'No, No'; anything more than this comes from the evil one."

MATTHEW 5:33–37

Elaborate incantations or vehement curses are alike futile. God cannot be manipulated by our use of language. Prayer, the opposite of swearing, is language put to the service of God. It is the simplest, and purest speech there is.

What scriptures does Jesus quote?

God, purge all pretense and affectation from my speech. I want all my words to be an offering in love, all my speech a servant of truth, in the ways that Jesus taught. Amen.

Love Your Enemies

"You have heard that it was said, 'An eye for an eye and a tooth for a tooth.' But I say to you, Do not resist an evildoer. But if anyone strikes you on the right cheek, turn the other also; and if anyone wants to sue you and take your coat, give your cloak as well; and if anyone forces you to go one mile, go also the second mile. Give to everyone who begs from you, and do not refuse anyone who wants to borrow from you.

"You have heard that it was said, 'You shall love your neighbor and hate your enemy.' But I say to you, Love your enemies and pray for those who persecute you, so that you may be children of your Father in heaven; for he makes his sun rise on the evil and on the good, and sends rain on the righteous and on the unrighteous. For if you love those who love you, what reward do you have? Do not even the tax collectors do the same? And if you greet only your brothers and sisters, what more are you doing than others?"

MATTHEW 5:38–47

Jesus commands a daring and courageous initiative that closes the gap between offender and offended. Love is not a reward to be parceled out as a favor to friends; it is a tactic by which we share the best in us so that others have an opportunity to live at their best.

Name an enemy you will love.

Christ of compassion, for too long I have let my emotions and my prejudices tell me who and how to love. No longer. I will go to school in your salvation and learn your way of love. Amen.

Perfect

"Be perfect, therefore, as your heavenly Father is perfect."

MATTHEW 5:48

When we abandon the way of knee-jerk ethics—mindlessly react-ing to the words and actions of others—we are free to become what love and grace stimulate in us: a wholeness that will finally be perfect.

Compare this with Ephesians 4:15–16.

Fashion in me what is obedient, eternal God, what is trusting and loving. Deal with what is rebellious, wayward, and misguided. I submit myself to your potter's hand. Amen.

Practicing Your Piety

"Beware of practicing your piety before others in order to be seen by them; for then you have no reward from your Father in heaven."

MATTHEW 6:1

The Christian who cares only for God's approval lives free of the tyranny of conformist pressures, relaxed under the steady direction of the God who loves us and gives himself for us. Those who try to please the world by their good behavior very quickly find themselves under the unkind surveillance of a thousand critics.

What behavior of yours is determined by what people think?

Make me indifferent, God, to the world's approval, but sensitive to yours. How easy it is to get enlisted in the piety parade! Keep me from pretense, from poses, from posturings. For Jesus's sake. Amen.

February 23

In Secret

"So whenever you give alms, do not sound a trumpet before you, as the hypocrites do in the synagogues and in the streets, so that they may be praised by others. Truly I tell you, they have received their reward. But when you give alms, do not let your left hand know what your right hand is doing, so that your alms may be done in secret; and your Father who sees in secret will reward you."

MATTHEW 6:2–4

When what is supposed to give aid to poor bodies becomes a means of aggrandizing proud spirits, piety is turned on its head. Nothing spoils acts of mercy and gifts of charity more quickly than publicity.

How do you guard the secrecy of your giving?

Father in heaven, lead me to speak in kindness and act in mercy unobtrusively and faithfully, just as you worked quietly and persistently behind the scenes in Jesus. Amen.

Like the Hypocrites

"And whenever you pray, do not be like the hypocrites; for they love to stand and pray in the synagogues and at the street corners, so that they may be seen by others. Truly I tell you, they have received their reward."

MATTHEW 6:5

Prayer that is used for any other purpose, no matter how lofty, than to personally converse with a personal God is a sham. It must never be used as a part of public relations. It must never be put to the services of creating a good image.

What is a hypocrite?

Free my spirit, God, from self-consciousness and self-righteousness. Forgive me for confusing the outward and the inward. Let my prayers be spontaneously honest and personally passionate. Amen.

When You Pray

"But whenever you pray, go into your room and shut the door and pray to your Father who is in secret; and your Father who sees in secret will reward you."

Matthew 6:6

The private room and the locked door diminish our tendencies to pose and strut; they also shut out distractions. Prayer is a conversation with God in which authenticity of spirit and attentiveness of mind are essential.

How do you get privacy in prayer?

"Father, in Thy mysterious presence kneeling, fain would our souls feel all Thy kindling love; for we are weak, and need some deep revealing of trust and strength and calmness from above." * Amen.

---

* Samuel Johnson, "Father, in Thy Mysterious Presence Kneeling," *The Hymnbook*, 326.

February 26

Empty Phrases

"When you are praying, do not heap up empty phrases as the Gentiles do; for they think that they will be heard because of their many words."

MATTHEW 6:7

"Knowledge of speech, but not of silence; Knowledge of words, and ignorance of the Word."* We live in an age of mass communication and minimal communion. When we have a good listener, we do not have to talk either a lot or loudly. God is a good listener.

Do you ever pray in empty phrases?

Holy Spirit, make the connection between the words of my mouth and the meanings in my heart so that my words may never be without personal meaning and my spirit never be without a means of expression. Amen.

* T. S. Eliot, "Choruses from 'The Rock,'" *The Waste Land and Other Poems* (London: Faber & Faber, 1972).

February 27

Knows What You Need

"Do not be like them, for your Father knows what you need before you ask him."

Matthew 6:8

Prayer is not a job list assigned by us to God. Nor is it a transfer of information between earth and heaven. God knows our condition and our needs. Prayer, like the best conversations on earth, cultivates intimacy, nurtures obedience, and becomes a way of working with God.

If God knows what you need, why pray?

In my prayers, O God, I will not make speeches to you, but learn a relationship with you. I want to express myself completely and listen to you devoutly, in Jesus's name and for his sake. Amen.

February 28

Pray Then in This Way

"Pray then in this way: Our Father in heaven, hallowed be your name. Your kingdom come. Your will be done, on earth as it is in heaven. Give us this day our daily bread. And forgive us our debts, as we also have forgiven our debtors. And do not bring us to the time of trial, but rescue us from the evil one."

MATTHEW 6:9–13

The act of praying is no uncharted wilderness where we hack and forge our way. It is well traveled, with rich traditions and deep culture. Jesus's words are compass and map for finding our way to the deep interiors.

Why is this prayer important to you?

"O Thou, by whom we come to God, the Life, the Truth, the Way; the path of Prayer Thyself hath trod; Lord, teach us how to pray!" * Amen.

* James Montgomery, "Prayer Is the Soul's Sincere Desire," *The Hymnbook*, 331.

_____

Father

"Pray then in this way: Our Father in heaven, hallowed be your name."

MATTHEW 6:9

"Our" is the operative word. We cannot come to God as if he were a private deity, a household god. He is no personal idol we manufacture to our specifications. In prayer God is not reduced to our requirements; we are expanded to the dimensions of his majesty.

Why is "father" such an important word for God?

Our Father: reveal yourself to me not as I have imagined you and not as others have stereotyped you, but as you really are: creator of all that is, loving redeemer of all your people. Amen.

Name

"Pray then in this way: Our Father in heaven, hallowed be your name."

MATTHEW 6:9

The word "God" comprises goodness and holiness and glory. But in everyday usage it is marred with superstition. People read into the word "God" fears and ignorance and blasphemy. The name needs cleansing and burnishing.

What does "hallowed" mean?

Hallowed be thy name: purge the words that name your presence, cleanse the images that fill my mind. Scrape the noun clean of rust and grime until "Jesus" and "Christ" say the clear truth about you, Father. Amen.

March 3

Kingdom

"Your kingdom come. Your will be done, on earth as it is in heaven."

MATTHEW 6:10

Every political scheme devised by humans is flawed somewhere, corrupt finally. The task of ordering people's lives in harmony and in fairness eludes our competence. Meanwhile, there are people who are already being ruled in love and who experience in that rule God's goodness and fulfillment.

What does "kingdom" mean?

Thy kingdom come: establish your principles of redemption in me and among all who kneel in your presence and confess your lordship. Inaugurate your rule, Lord Jesus, and make me a charter citizen. Amen.

March 4

Will

"Your kingdom come. Your will be done, on earth as it is in heaven."

Matthew 6:10

Our wills are given to us to exercise freely. We can assert them noisily and brashly, like Adam, in choosing what is beneath us and thereby being diminished; or we can choose, like Christ, the way of our creator and redeemer and learn a greater freedom in an expanding reality.

How does your will differ from God's will?

Thy will be done: the will that freely elects redemption in your creation, the will that comprehends all things and everyone in a divine purpose, the will that frees my will from slavery to sin and puts it to work in righteousness. Amen.

March 5

Give

"Give us this day our daily bread."

MATTHEW 6:11

God created our bodily as well as our spiritual hungers, and will provide for their satisfaction. Prayer has as much to do with the necessities of this day's living as with the certainties of eternal life.

What physical needs will you pray for today?

Give us this day our daily bread. I will not let my needs become anxieties, but will submit them to your providence. Give, Lord, all that I need to live obediently and joyously. Amen.

Forgive

"And forgive us our debts, as we also have forgiven our debtors."

MATTHEW 6:12

Apart from forgiveness each step we take is a link in the cause-and-effect sequence of sin and death. With forgiveness we travel from "strength to strength" by grace to life eternal. In the same way that bread is a basic need for the body, forgiveness is the basic need of the spirit.

Who can you forgive as you have been forgiven?

Forgive us our debts as we forgive our debtors: I want each detail of my life to be a result not of the sins I commit, but of the mercy you pour out in Jesus. Don't, God, ignore me, indulge me, or reject me. Forgive me. Amen.

March 7

Rescue

"And do not bring us to the time of trial, but rescue us from the evil one."

MATTHEW 6:13

Christians are not moral giants, flexing our muscles and displaying our trophies before the world as evidence of superior spirituality. We are in a battle that very often threatens to overwhelm us, and we need help.

What evil do you need help against?

Lead us not into temptation, but deliver us from evil: I thank you, God, that you are not coolly manipulating me, puppet-like, on a string; but that you are with me, on my side in this war for eternal life, and that you will bring the victory. Amen.

March 8

Kingdom/Power/Glory

"And do not bring us to the time of trial, but rescue us from the evil one."

MATTHEW 6:13

These words, though not in the oldest manuscripts, are commonly on the lips of Christians. They summarize prayer as the language spoken in God's kingdom, voiced with energy given by God's power, and however stuttering, resplendent with God's glory.

How does the Lord's Prayer help you to pray?

Thine is the kingdom and the power and the glory, forever: all that you are, O God, evokes and shapes my prayers to you. Keep me in the company of all who are struggling to master this tongue. Help me to be articulate in this great language. Amen.

March 9

If You Forgive

"For if you forgive others their trespasses, your heavenly Father will also forgive you; but if you do not forgive others, neither will your Father forgive your trespasses."

MATTHEW 6:14–15

God's work includes our neighbors, and we must join him in it if we are to continue in his ways. We are always trying to reduce God's work to something exclusive and private, but he will not permit it.

Whom will you forgive today?

At first, Lord, these words look like a posted warning, but now I see in them a way of promise—your words of forgiveness spill out into the world through my acts of forgiveness. Thank you for letting me share in your great and creative work of forgiving. Amen.

March 10

Do Not Look Dismal

"And whenever you fast, do not look dismal, like the hypocrites, for they disfigure their faces so as to show others that they are fasting. Truly I tell you, they have received their reward. But when you fast, put oil on your head and wash your face, so that your fasting may be seen not by others but by your Father who is in secret; and your Father who sees in secret will reward you."

Matthew 6:16–18

Routines dull perceptions. The purpose of a discipline such as fasting is to interrupt the routines that cushion us from the foundational realities, and so sharpen our awareness of the eternal essentials.

Will you choose a day, or a meal, to fast this week?

Lord God, I let too many things distract and divert me from paying attention to you: train me in the simplifications that will put me in touch with what matters most—your love, your salvation, your grace. Amen.

March 11

Treasures

"Do not store up for yourselves treasures on earth, where moth and rust consume and where thieves break in and steal; but store up for yourselves treasures in heaven, where neither moth nor rust consumes and where thieves do not break in and steal. For where your treasure is, there your heart will be also."

MATTHEW 6:19–21

God has nothing against treasure; his concern is about its location. The location of our treasure, that upon which we expend energy and fix hopes, determines the direction of our goals and the shape of our behavior.

What do you value most?

Father, I put all my wealth, my investments, my possessions in trust: you are my future and my confidence. Cure me of the possessiveness that holds tightly and will not let go. Amen.

March 12

If Your Eye Is Healthy

"The eye is the lamp of the body. So, if your eye is healthy, your whole body will be full of light; but if your eye is unhealthy, your whole body will be full of darkness. If then the light in you is darkness, how great is the darkness!"

MATTHEW 6:22–23

Our eyes are remarkable and accurate signs of our inner spiritual health. They narrow into slits when we hate, envy, and scheme. They open wide in wonder when we live in adoration and generosity.

What obstructs your vision of God?

God, your world is so full of people to love and things to admire: keep my eyes wide open to receive all the sensations of color and form in your creation, and to love everything and everyone I see in Jesus's name. Amen.

March 13

Two Masters

"No one can serve two masters; for a slave will either hate the one and love the other, or be devoted to the one and despise the other. You cannot serve God and wealth."

MATTHEW 6:24

Faith is not an amalgam of all the bits and pieces of "religion" that are deposited in the delta of the soul. The Christian is not a collection bin for every religious emotion that passes through the nervous system. Christian faith is choice and service—choosing Christ as Savior and serving him as Lord.

How would you serve "wealth"?

I know, God, that I cannot trust you as just another item in the religious stew I keep simmering on the back burner of my life. Master me absolutely so that I may serve you in body, mind, and spirit, as I now attend to your word of creation and command in Jesus Christ. Amen.

March 14

Do Not Worry

"Therefore I tell you, do not worry about your life, what you will eat or what you will drink, or about your body, what you will wear. Is not life more than food, and the body more than clothing? Look at the birds of the air; they neither sow nor reap nor gather into barns, and yet your heavenly Father feeds them. Are you not of more value than they?"

MATTHEW 6:25–26

Survival needs, important as they are, must not be allowed to define or dominate us. We are created for something far more complex and profound than food and drink and clothing. God's love, care, and providence are the wide world in which we learn to live easily and exuberantly.

What anxiety will you turn over to God?

Father in heaven, forgetful of my high calling in Christ, I find myself flattened out on an economic plain, living from hand to mouth with a mean, survival mentality. Awaken the desire to live by your will, as your child, in your love. Amen.

March 15

A Single Hour

"And can any of you by worrying add a single hour to your span of
life?"

MATTHEW 6:27

Anxiety burns up enormous amounts of energy, wastefully and
inefficiently. It produces nothing. It is the opposite of faith, which
requires only plain attentiveness to God, and simple responses to
his will—and moves mountains.

Compare anxiety with the faith described in Hebrews 11:1.

*Lord Jesus Christ, you have so richly and extravagantly provided me with
meaning and purpose and beauty and goodness—what more do I want?
Teach me to live in the amplitude of your creation, not in the grab-greed
desolation of the world. Amen.*

March 16

Little Faith

"And can any of you by worrying add a single hour to your span of life? And why do you worry about clothing? Consider the lilies of the field, how they grow; they neither toil nor spin, yet I tell you, even Solomon in all his glory was not clothed like one of these. But if God so clothes the grass of the field, which is alive today and tomorrow is thrown into the oven, will he not much more clothe you—you of little faith?"

MATTHEW 6:27–30

Anxious preoccupation with the needs and wants of daily living distract us from God, who is already present in each detail to help, strengthen, provide, and redeem by his love.

Compare this with the other "little faith" passages in Matthew 8:26; 14:31; and 16:8.

Dear Christ, I set aside right now my nervous concern for what I must do; I center my thoughts on what you are doing in me and in the world. I want to trade in my anxieties for your gift of faith. Amen.

March 17

Your Heavenly Father Knows

"Therefore do not worry, saying, 'What will we eat?' or 'What will we drink?' or 'What will we wear?' For it is the Gentiles who strive for all these things; and indeed your heavenly Father knows that you need all these things."

MATTHEW 6:31–32

Faith breathes a confidence that God knows our needs better than we do and provides for their fulfillment. The frantic doubt that God may have forgotten about us, the panicky suspicion that God may have decided against us—all that is excluded by faith.

What are you most sure of in God?

For your uninterrupted mercy, O God, for the constant surveillance of your provident eye, for the steady assistance of your strong arm, for the persistent invitational knocking at the door of my life, for these I give thanks. Amen.

March 18

Strive First

"But strive first for the kingdom of God and his righteousness, and all these things will be given to you as well."

MATTHEW 6:33

Our priorities should be clear by now: We are made by God, for God; therefore the meaning and fulfillment of our lives must take place in the country of grace. What he says and what he does, and how we respond and how we obey, are the center realities of our lives.

What evidence is there in your life that you seek first his kingdom?

"Be still, my soul: the Lord is on thy side; bear patiently the cross of grief or pain; leave to thy God to order and provide; in every change He faithful will remain. Be still, my soul: thy best, thy heavenly Friend through thorny ways leads to a joyful end." * Amen.

---

* Katherina von Schlegel, "Be Still My Soul," *The Hymnbook*, 318.

March 19

So Do Not Worry

"But strive first for the kingdom of God and his righteousness, and all these things will be given to you as well. So do not worry about tomorrow, for tomorrow will bring worries of its own. Today's trouble is enough for today."

MATTHEW 6:33–34

If we are in control of what happens to us and in charge of our own well-being, we do well to be perpetually vigilant against evil and on constant alert for the lucky break. But if God is in control, if his kingdom is already a reality, a decisive "therefore" separates us from such debilitating anxieties.

What do you seek first?

My God and King: in the course of this day, as I am presented with choices to make and paths to follow, give me the wise courage to decide to live in the Kingdom where I will experience your power and glory in Jesus Christ. Amen.

March 20

Do Not Judge

"Do not judge, so that you may not be judged. For with the judgment you make you will be judged, and the measure you give will be the measure you get. For with the judgment you make you will be judged, and the measure you give will be the measure you get."

MATTHEW 7:1–2

When we judge others—evaluate their worth, their lack of virtue, their practice of vice—we waste the moral energies that were given to us for use in the work of compassion. Examining others with an eye to spotting their defects is self-destructive.

Whom are you tempted to judge?

I find, by your word, O God, that I am utterly incompetent to judge others. I have only meager information about them; I only vaguely understand your purposes in them. Instead of pronouncing judgments on them, I will work and pray for them, in Jesus's name. Amen.

March 21

The Speck/The Log

"Why do you see the speck in your neighbor's eye, but do not notice the log in your own eye? Or how can you say to your neighbor, 'Let me take the speck out of your eye,' while the log is in your own eye? You hypocrite, first take the log out of your own eye, and then you will see clearly to take the speck out of your neighbor's eye."

MATTHEW 7:3–5

Not until we refuse to indulge our curiosity about what is wrong with others are we free to take a genuine interest in them as people loved by God to whom we may become witnesses in truth and companions in faith. Too many times we confuse religious gossip with spiritual concern.

Whom are you judging instead of loving?

Lord, bring me to the place where my interest is not in condemning sin in others, but in confessing it in myself. I find it much easier to mount an indignant assault on everyone else's sins than to repent and be cleansed of my own. Amen.

March 22

Pearls Before Swine

"Do not give what is holy to dogs; and do not throw your pearls before swine, or they will trample them under foot and turn and maul you."

MATTHEW 7:6

Our Lord leads us in knowing when to speak and act, just as he teaches us what is to be done and spoken. Timing is important in witnessing and helping, teaching and preaching. "Readiness is all."*

What good deeds have you done in the wrong place?

Holy Spirit, give me the gift of discerning hearts and being sensitive to needs, so that as I share the truth and goodness of my Lord, I may not provoke rejection by my rudeness nor encourage irreverence by my ignorance. For Jesus's sake. Amen.

* Shakespeare, *Hamlet*, act 5, scene 2, line 232.

March 23

Ask

"Ask, and it will be given you; search, and you will find; knock, and the door will be opened for you."

MATTHEW 7:7

When we ask we admit our inadequacy and confess God's sufficiency. Asking is the basic prayer. In such prayer connections are soldered between our brokenness and his wholeness.

What will you ask from God today?

Great God, consummate all my desires in your love; complete all my wants in your grace. Thank you for the invitation and the promise: the invitation to put all my needs before you, the promise that you will meet them in wisdom and peace. Amen.

March 24

... Do So to Them

"In everything do to others as you would have them do to you; for this is the law and the prophets."

MATTHEW 7:12

The most remarkable thing about this summary sentence on behavior is not in the words themselves but in the life—commentary that Jesus provided. This is what he did. He converted all morality from wish to reality, from ideal to actuality. And what he did he enables us to do.

How can you use this golden rule in a specific action?

"So let our lips and lives express the holy gospel we profess; so let our works and virtues shine, to prove the doctrine all divine. Thus shall we best proclaim abroad the honors of our Savior God, when His salvation reigns within, and grace subdues the power of sin." * Amen.

---

* Isaac Watts, "So Let Our Lips and Lives Express," *The Hymnbook,* 250.

March 25

The Narrow Gate

"Enter through the narrow gate; for the gate is wide and the road is easy that leads to destruction, and there are many who take it. For the gate is narrow and the road is hard that leads to life, and there are few who find it."

MATTHEW 7:13–14

Faith is not an accumulation of vague impulses that tend, generally, toward the good, nor is it the nurture of obscure emotions of piety; it is choosing to walk through a particular gate ("I am the door" [John 10:7]), and down a definite road ("I am the way" [John 14:6]).

What do you find difficult or demanding about the narrow gate?

Lord Jesus, you are my way and my truth and my life. Lead me through the narrow gate into the wide life, through the place of concentrated decision into the country of expansive blessings Amen.

March 26

Beware of False Prophets

"Beware of false prophets, who come to you in sheep's clothing but inwardly are ravenous wolves."

MATTHEW 7:15

Christian charity must not be confused with pious gullibility that puts up with fraud and nonsense in its leaders. Religious claims are the easiest to make, but the hardest to document, Prophetic mantles easily assumed must be painstakingly verified.

How do you exercise caution toward religious leaders?

Give me, Lord, the gift of discernment so that I may not be led astray by those who prey upon my faith, so that I may not be exploited by those who would profit from my devotion. For Jesus's sake. Amen.

Fruits

"You will know them by their fruits. Are grapes gathered from thorns, or figs from thistles? In the same way, every good tree bears good fruit, but the bad tree bears bad fruit. A good tree cannot bear bad fruit, nor can a bad tree bear good fruit. Every tree that does not bear good fruit is cut down and thrown into the fire. Thus you will know them by their fruits."

MATTHEW 7:16–20

In evaluating religious leadership, it is far more useful to observe how a person treats his dog than to ask him for his opinions on God. "Fruits" are not success anecdotes or upward-swinging statistical curves, but instances in which it is obvious that inward belief has metamorphosed into behavior.

What fruits do you see in your spiritual leaders?

Father, I don't want to be uncritically naive toward someone just because he or she is called pastor, or preacher, or evangelist; but neither do I want to develop a cynical skepticism toward anyone who is in the spotlight. Show me the middle way of alert obedience in and through Jesus Christ. Amen.

March 28

Lord, Lord

"Not everyone who says to me, "Lord, Lord," will enter the kingdom of heaven, but only the one who does the will of my Father in heaven. On that day many will say to me, 'Lord, Lord, did we not prophesy in your name, and cast out demons in your name, and do many deeds of power in your name?' Then I will declare to them, 'I never knew you; go away from me, you evildoers.'"

MATTHEW 7:21–23

Name-dropping works the same way in spiritual things as it does in earthly things—it gives the impression of intimacy when there is only the flimsiest of relationships. Using the name will get us nowhere if we are unrelated to the person we name.

Are you a religious name—dropper?

Lord Christ, when I use your name, keep me honest so that I am expressing a relationship with you and engaging in a response to your will. I want my whole life, not just my mouth, to speak your name. Amen.

March 29

Founded on the Rock

"Everyone then who hears these words of mine and acts on them will be like a wise man who built his house on rock. The rain fell, the floods came, and the winds blew and beat on that house, but it did not fall, because it had been founded on rock. And everyone who hears these words of mine and does not act on them will be like a foolish man who built his house on sand. The rain fell, and the floods came, and the winds blew and beat against that house, and it fell—and great was its fall!"

MATTHEW 7:24–27

Visible behavior is built on invisible truth. Jesus provides the commands that, as we obey them, are solid, foundational underpinnings for eternal life.

What are some items in your life foundation?

All praise to you, O God, for giving me such weighty, sure, foundation-making commands. Thank you for giving me the desire to respond to them in obedient belief. Give me daily directions for building upon Christ the rock. Amen.

March 30

"Astounded at His Teaching"

Now when Jesus had finished saying these things, the crowds were astounded at his teaching, for he taught them as one having authority, and not as their scribes.

Matthew 7:28–29

The world is so full of people who attempt to shock, startle, and surprise us that we finally become blase. Then our Lord comes along and speaks the truth simply and truly. The sheer authenticity and naked reality of it shakes us out of our ennui.

What is most astonishing to you in Jesus's words?

"My hope is built on nothing less than Jesus's blood and righteousness; I dare not trust the sweetest frame, but wholly lean on Jesus's name. On Christ, the solid rock, I stand; all other ground is sinking sand."* Amen.

---

* E. Mote, "My Hope Is Built on Nothing Less," *The Hymnbook,* 313.

March 31

"Lord, If You Choose"

When Jesus had come down from the mountain, great crowds followed him; and there was a leper who came to him and knelt before him, saying, "Lord, if you choose, you can make me clean." He stretched out his hand and touched him, saying, "I do choose. Be made clean!" Immediately his leprosy was cleansed. Then Jesus said to him, "See that you say nothing to anyone; but go, show yourself to the priest, and offer the gift that Moses commanded, as a testimony to them."

MATTHEW 8:1–4

The leper is the needy person in extremis: cut off, lonely, shunned. But no needy condition is so extreme or so absolute that we are consigned to despair. There is hope in God. The approach, timid and tentative—"if you will"—unexpectedly finds a bold and positive desire to save: "I will."

What was so bad about being a leper?

I want cleansing, dear Christ, quite as much as that leper. But in your way; what you will. I want my life to be shaped not by my demands, but by the sure but mysterious movement of your grace. Amen.

April 1

Only Speak the Word

When he entered Capernaum, a centurion came to him, ... "Lord, my servant is lying at home paralyzed, in terrible distress." And he said to him, "I will come and cure him." The centurion answered, "Lord, I am not worthy to have you come under my roof; but only speak the word, and my servant will be healed. For I also am a man under authority, with soldiers under me; and I say to one, 'Go,' and he goes. . . ." When Jesus heard him, he was amazed and said to those who followed him, "Truly I tell you, in no one in Israel have I found such faith. . . ." And to the centurion Jesus said, "Go; let it be done for you according to your faith." And the servant was healed in that hour.

MATTHEW 8:5–13

The centurion did what he knew best; he used everyday experience (his military training) to gain access to the operations of God. Faith, in this case, is not an extraordinary leap into the unknown, but a commonplace step into what was clear and present in Jesus.

Whom do you want Jesus to help?

Christ, there are so many paralyzed people around, so many servant-children helpless apart from you. Help them. I can't help them; I only run to you and announce the "terrible distresses" to which you are neither impotent nor indifferent. Amen.

April 2

Nowhere to Lay His Head

When Jesus entered Peter's house, he saw his mother-in-law lying in bed with a fever; he touched her hand, and the fever left her, and she got up and began to serve him. That evening they brought to him many who were possessed with demons; and he cast out the spirits with a word, and cured all who were sick. This was to fulfill what had been spoken through the prophet Isaiah, "He took our infirmities and bore our diseases." Now when Jesus saw great crowds around him, he gave orders to go over to the other side. A scribe then approached and said, "Teacher, I will follow you wherever you go." And Jesus said to him, "Foxes have holes, and birds of the air have nests; but the Son of Man has nowhere to lay his head." Another of his disciples said to him, "Lord, first let me go and bury my father." But Jesus said to him, "Follow me, and let the dead bury their own dead."

MATTHEW 8:14–22

Jesus responds to our desire for a closer walk with him by reading us the fine print of disciple-ship: a loss of creature comforts ("the foxes have holes ...") and a setting aside of old priorities ("let the dead bury the dead").

How does Christ change your values?

I want to go where you go, Jesus. I think I am willing to do anything. Then you confront me with where you are going and what you are doing, and I am not so sure. Give me, along with the desire to be with you, the courage to stay with you. Amen.

April 3

Little Faith

And when he got into the boat, his disciples followed him.

Matthew 8:23–27

A windstorm arose on the sea, so great that the boat was being swamped by the waves; but he was asleep. And they went and woke him up, saying, "Lord, save us! We are perishing!" And he said to them, "Why are you afraid, you of little faith?" Then he got up and rebuked the winds and the sea; and there was a dead calm. They were amazed, saying, "What sort of man is this, that even the winds and the sea obey him?"

By this time these disciples should have known who they were with, and what happens when they are with him. But they are more worried about the weather than they are trustful of their savior.

Would you have been afraid?

My goal, Savior Christ, is to believe in you so deeply and throughly that my first response in every crisis is faith in what you will do, trust in how you will bless. But I have a long way to go. Lead me from my fearful midget-faith to mature adulthood. Amen.

April 4

They Begged Him to Leave

When he came to the other side, to the country of the Gadarenes, two demoniacs coming out of the tombs met him. They were so fierce that no one could pass that way. Suddenly they shouted, "What have you to do with us, Son of God? Have you come here to torment us before the time?" Now a large herd of swine was feeding at some distance from them. The demons begged him, "If you cast us out, send us into the herd of swine." And he said to them, "Go!" So they came out and entered the swine; and suddenly, the whole herd rushed down the steep bank into the sea and perished in the water. The swineherds ran off, and on going into the town, they told the whole story about what had happened to the demoniacs. Then the whole town came out to meet Jesus; and when they saw him, they begged him to leave.

MATTHEW 8:28–34

In Gadara, property was valued more highly than people. That two people were restored to sanity was a triviality compared to the loss of their pigs. They wanted nothing to do with Jesus if it meant they had more people to love and less property to hold.

What does Jesus do to your value system?

Where are my values, Lord Jesus? I pay lip service to the priorities of people, but I give an enormous amount of time and attention to things. Examine me carefully; if there is any possession that is making it impossible for me to love people and praise you for your work in them, show me how to get rid of it. Amen.

April 5

Your Sins Are Forgiven

And after getting into a boat he crossed the sea and came to his own town. And just then some people were carrying a paralyzed man lying on a bed. When Jesus saw their faith, he said to the paralytic, "Take heart, son; your sins are forgiven." Then some of the scribes said to themselves, "This man is blaspheming." But Jesus, perceiving their thoughts, said, "Why do you think evil in your hearts? For which is easier, to say, 'Your sins are forgiven,' or to say, 'Stand up and walk'? But so that you may know that the Son of Man has authority on earth to forgive sins"—he then said to the paralytic—"Stand up, take your bed and go to your home." And he stood up and went to his home. When the crowds saw it, they were filled with awe, and they glorified God, who had given such authority to human beings.

MATTHEW 9:1–8

Everyone, both the man and his friends, thought his basic need was physical. How surprised they were to hear Jesus address the invisible spiritual need. Jesus gets around to the physical, but he begins with his heart.

What do you think of as your most pressing need?

God, I wish for and pray for many noble things that are secondary and peripheral. My agenda of petition lacks theology—I fail to see my life in relation primarily to you. Deal with my needs as you see them. Get to my center and save me. Amen.

April 6

Follow Me

As Jesus was walking along, he saw a man called Matthew sitting at the tax booth; and he said to him, "Follow me." And he got up and followed him.

Matthew 9:9

God in Jesus addresses us by a personal name and with a personal command. He does not impersonally recruit us as workers or functionaries. When we respond we move out of a life in which what we do or others do is the main thing, and into a life where God is the controlling center.

What do you know about tax collectors?

"Follow, I would follow Thee, my Lord, follow every passing day. My tomorrows are all known to Thee, Thou wilt lead me all the way." * Amen.

---

* Anonymous.

April 7

Mercy, and Not Sacrifice

And as he sat at dinner in the house, many tax collectors and sinners came and were sitting with him and his disciples. When the Pharisees saw this, they said to his disciples, "Why does your teacher eat with tax collectors and sinners?" But when he heard this, he said, "Those who are well have no need of a physician, but those who are sick. Go and learn what this means, 'I desire mercy, not sacrifice.' For I have come to call not the righteous but sinners."

MATTHEW 9:10–13

The key word here is mercy—the divine will and energy of helping the hurt and saving the lost. It is set in contrast to sacrifice—the human attempt to arrange appearances so that they are pleasing to God.

How do Jesus's words change your outlook on life?

When I see things from your point of view, Lord Jesus, though everything is the same, everything is different: life is lived in grateful response to your mercy, not in obsessive and fearful attempts to look good. I can relax. I can praise. I can live to your glory. Amen.

April 8

Fresh Wineskins

Then the disciples of John came to him, saying, "Why do we and the Pharisees fast often, but your disciples do not fast?" And Jesus said to them, "The wedding guests cannot mourn as long as the bridegroom is with them, can they? The days will come when the bridegroom is taken away from them, and then they will fast. No one sews a piece of unshrunk cloth on an old cloak, for the patch pulls away from the cloak, and a worse tear is made. Neither is new wine put into old wineskins; otherwise, the skins burst, and the wine is spilled, and the skins are destroyed; but new wine is put into fresh wineskins, and so both are preserved."

MATTHEW 9:14–17

Fasting was, and is, a noble religious discipline. But fasting was not an end in itself, to be gradually perfected through the centuries, but preparation for a feast: and now the feast was served!

Do you ever confuse preparation with fulfillment?

Father in heaven, keep me flexible and responsive to your presence in my life, so that I will be ready at any moment to stop what I am doing in getting ready for you, and go with you in service or in praise, in witness or in celebration. Amen.

April 9

Daughter

While he was saying these things to them, suddenly a leader of the synagogue came in and knelt before him, saying, "My daughter has just died; but come and lay your hand on her, and she will live." And Jesus got up and followed him, with his disciples. Then suddenly a woman who had been suffering from hemorrhages for twelve years came up behind him and touched the fringe of his cloak, for she said to herself, "If I only touch his cloak, I will be made well." Jesus turned, and seeing her he said, "Take heart, daughter; your faith has made you well." And instantly the woman was made well. When Jesus came to the leader's house and saw the flute players and the crowd making a commotion, he said, "Go away; for the girl is not dead but sleeping." And they laughed at him. But when the crowd had been put outside, he went in and took her by the hand, and the girl got up.

MATTHEW 9:18–25

The two daughters, the one twelve years old, and the other twelve years sick, have their stories held together. The anonymous woman in the crowd gets healed with the same attentive tenderness as the daughter of the most prominent man in town.

What comparisons and contrasts do you see between the two?

When, Lord, will I learn the grand and ever freshly documented truth— no one is beneath your attention, no person is beyond your help. Keep me from the sin of despair, always ready for your resurrection word. Amen.

April 10

Two Blind Men

As Jesus went on from there, two blind men followed him, crying loudly, "Have mercy on us, Son of David!" When he entered the house, the blind men came to him; and Jesus said to them, "Do you believe that I am able to do this?" They said to him, "Yes, Lord." Then he touched their eyes and said, "According to your faith let it be done to you." And their eyes were opened. Then Jesus sternly ordered them, "See that no one knows of this." But they went away and spread the news about him throughout that district.

MATTHEW 9:27–31

The two blind men are typical of many: they enjoy immensely the benefits of being with Jesus, but blithely ignore his commands. As long as they need help, they are all eagerness and attention; as soon as they get what they came for, they disregard Jesus completely.

Why did the healed men disobey Jesus's command for silence?

Jesus Christ, I want to take your words to me just as seriously and personally as I do your acts for me. I need your help, but I also need your direction. Lead me from the faith that responds to your mercy into the faith that becomes obedient discipleship. Amen.

April 11

The Harvest Is Plentiful

After they had gone away, a demoniac who was mute was brought
to him. And when the demon had been cast out, the one who had
been mute spoke; and the crowds were amazed and said, "Never has
anything like this been seen in Israel." But the Pharisees said, "By
the ruler of the demons he casts out the demons." Then Jesus went
about all the cities and villages, teaching in their synagogues, and
proclaiming the good news of the kingdom, and curing every disease
and every sickness. When he saw the crowds, he had compassion for
them, because they were harassed and helpless, like sheep without a
shepherd. Then he said to his disciples, "The harvest is plentiful, but
the laborers are few; therefore ask the Lord of the harvest to send out
laborers into his harvest.

MATTHEW 9:32–38

To this point in the narrative, the emphasis has been on the ministry of Jesus. Now there is a transition as he enlists others in the
work of compassion. Jesus not only helps us, he helps us to help
others.

Where do you see a plentiful harvest?

*"Come, labor on, who dares stand idle on the harvest plain while all
around him waves the golden grain? And to each servant does the Master
say, Go work today"* * Amen.

* Jane Laurie Borthwick, "Come, Labor On," *The Hymnbook*, 248.

April 12

Give Without Payment

Then Jesus summoned his twelve disciples and gave them authority over unclean spirits, to cast them out, and to cure every disease and every sickness. . . . These twelve Jesus sent out with the following instructions: "Go nowhere among the Gentiles, and enter no town of the Samaritans, but go rather to the lost sheep of the house of Israel. As you go, proclaim the good news, 'The kingdom of heaven has come near. Cure the sick, raise the dead, cleanse the lepers, cast out demons. You received without payment; give without payment. Take no gold, or silver, or copper in your belts, no bag for your journey, or two tunics, or sandals, or a staff; for laborers deserve their food."

MATTHEW 10:1–10

We don't just receive Christ's ministry, we share it. Each Christian is a nexus for grace, an intersection of redemptive traffic. All the vigorous energies of joy (preaching), intelligence (teaching), and health (healing) spill out of our lives into the world.

What kind of ministry are you good at?

The sound of your commands, dear Christ, continues to ring in my ears: preach, heal, raise, cleanse, cast out. May all the love I experience from you get acted out in my encounters with the people I meet today. Amen.

April 13

Shake Off the Dust

"Whatever town or village you enter, find out who in it is worthy, and stay there until you leave. As you enter the house, greet it. If the house is worthy, let your peace come upon it; but if it is not worthy, let your peace return to you. If anyone will not welcome you or listen to your words, shake off the dust from your feet as you leave that house or town. Truly I tell you, it will be more tolerable for the land of Sodom and Gomorrah on the day of judgment than for that town."

MATTHEW 10:11–15

Ministry is not ingratiation. We must not conduct our lives of service so that people will like us; for if we do, we only become a servant to the neurotic needs of others, not a witness to the healthy promises of God.

How does it feel to have your witness rejected?

My commitment, Lord, is to you—not to success at any cost, not to acceptance by everyone. Keep me loyal, obeying your commands and doing your work, more interested in being faithful than in being popular. Amen.

April 14

Before the Son of Man Comes

"See, I am sending you out like sheep into the midst of wolves; so be wise as serpents and innocent as doves. Beware of them, for they will hand you over to councils and flog you in their synagogues, and you will be dragged before governors and kings because of me, as a testimony to them and the Gentiles. When they hand you over, do not worry about how you are to speak or what you are to say; for what you are to say will be given to you at that time; for it is not you who speak, but the Spirit of your Father speaking through you. Brother will betray brother to death, and a father his child, and children will rise against parents and have them put to death; and you will be hated by all because of my name. But the one who endures to the end will be saved. When they persecute you in one town, flee to the next; for truly I tell you, you will not have gone through all the towns of Israel before the Son of Man comes."

MATTHEW 10:16–23

We live, spiritually and morally, in hostile country. We need to be realistic about that. What we must not do is write doomsday endings to this experience. Family strife, social discord, church unrest are not the end. Christ is the end.

What hostility do you experience?

In each obstacle I meet today, Savior Christ, I will look for your help, anticipate your coming. Show me how to live in hard times with a light heart. Amen.

April 15

How Much More

"A disciple is not above the teacher, nor a slave above the master; it is enough for the disciple to be like the teacher, and the slave like the master. If they have called the master of the house Beelzebul, how much more will they malign those of his household!"

MATTHEW 10:24–25

We don't mind suffering for things we do that deserve punishment; but when we suffer for doing the right, we mind terribly. But that is exactly what we let ourselves in for as Christ's disciples—misapprehension and rejection in pursuit of the good.

In what ways do people misunderstand you?

Lord Jesus Christ, I want to understand exactly the ways in which you expressed the truth, and want to patiently submit myself to experiencing that way of life, not trying to get out of the hard parts, not complaining about the unpopularity, but enduring and faithful. Amen.

April 16

You Are of More Value

"So have no fear of them; for nothing is covered up that will not be uncovered, and nothing secret that will not become known. What I say to you in the dark, tell in the light; and what you hear whispered, proclaim from the housetops. Do not fear those who kill the body but cannot kill the soul; rather fear him who can destroy both soul and body in hell. Are not two sparrows sold for a penny? Yet not one of them will fall to the ground apart from your Father. And even the hairs of your head are all counted. So do not be afraid; you are of more value than many sparrows. Everyone therefore who acknowledges me before others, I also will acknowledge before my Father in heaven;"

MATTHEW 10:26–32

In Christ's kingdom no person is subordinated to a principle or a cause, used as a case history in a dissertation on goodness or sin. We are not treated as a means to anything; we are valued for who we are.

How many times does the word "fear" occur here?

When I look, Lord, at what other people do and say I become fearful— and rightly so, for my life to them is merely something to manipulate. But when I listen to what you say and believe in what you are doing, I trust, sure that revelation will triumph over hiddenness and resurrection over destruction. Amen.

April 17

Not Worthy

"But whoever denies me before others, I also will deny before my Father in heaven. Do not think that I have come to bring peace to the earth; I have not come to bring peace, but a sword. For I have come to set a man against his father, and a daughter against her mother, and a daughter-in-law against her mother-in-law; and one's foes will be members of one's own household. Whoever loves father or mother more than me is not worthy of me; and whoever loves son or daughter more than me is not worthy of me; and whoever does not take up the cross and follow me is not worthy of me. Those who find their life will lose it, and those who lose their life for my sake will find it."

MATTHEW 10:33–39

We commonly avoid conflicts and encounters that require decisions between the good and the best, between the convenient and the excellent. We sink into a quagmire of domesticity, security, and self-gratification. The result is a conglomerate arrangement of habits and associations that we misname "community," sometimes even "church." But Christ has something far better.

What does Christ's sword do?

Better your sword, Lord, than the world's peace. I want the clarity of sharp decisions, not the amoral smog of confused compromises. Separate me from the half-gods of this world; free me for total response to you. Amen.

April 18

A Cup of Cold Water

"Whoever welcomes you welcomes me, and whoever welcomes me welcomes the one who sent me. Whoever welcomes a prophet in the name of a prophet will receive a prophet's reward; and whoever welcomes a righteous person in the name of a righteous person will receive the reward of the righteous; and whoever gives even a cup of cold water to one of these little ones in the name of a disciple—truly I tell you, none of these will lose their reward."

MATTHEW 10:40–42

Our acceptance of others and our service to others does not have to agonize over who is worthy, over what takes priority: Christ is present in everyone, everywhere. Our acts of trust and compassion, of witness and help, are anticipated by his, and fulfilled in his.

Who are some of the "little ones" in your life?

I dream, Father, of doing great acts of service in your name; meanwhile there are little opportunities for help all around us. Keep me faithful in the small tasks, discovering your presence in overlooked people and in obscure places. Amen.

April 19

Are We to Wait?

Now when Jesus had finished instructing his twelve disciples, he went on from there to teach and proclaim his message in their cities. When John heard in prison what the Messiah was doing, he sent word by his disciples, and said to him, "Are you the one who is to come, or are we to wait for another?" Jesus answered them, "Go and tell John what you hear and see: the blind receive their sight, the lame walk, the lepers are cleansed, the deaf hear, the dead are raised, and the poor have good news brought to them. And blessed is anyone who takes no offense at me."

MATTHEW 11:1–6

Jesus doesn't get popular applause for what he does, he doesn't overwhelmingly convince everyone of his truth. Even John, who prepared the way for Jesus's ministry, has his doubts. God in Christ doesn't come among us to meet our expectations, but to save us from our sins.

Why do you think John was in doubt about Jesus?

I have a lot of questions, Lord God, especially when things aren't going well in my life. I wonder if you are doing your job, if you have included me in your plans. And then, by faith, I get a larger vision, comprehend a deeper hope, and bless you for your mysterious and glorious work. Amen.

April 20

What Then Did You Go out to See?

As they went away, Jesus began to speak to the crowds about John: "What did you go out into the wilderness to look at? A reed shaken by the wind? What then did you go out to see? Someone dressed in soft robes? Look, those who wear soft robes are in royal palaces. What then did you go out to see? A prophet? Yes, I tell you, and more than a prophet. This is the one about whom it is written, 'See, I am sending my messenger ahead of you, who will prepare your way before you.' Truly I tell you, among those born of women no one has arisen greater than John the Baptist; yet the least in the kingdom of heaven is greater than he."

MATTHEW 11:7–11

Are we tourists, sightseeing in religion with binoculars and camera? Do we reduce the man of God to a spectacle? But the gospel is not a spectator sport; it is not window-shopping. God's rule has already broken in. The participation of the least, not the fame of the great, is what is important.

Why was John important?

It is a lot easier for me, Lord Jesus, to be an onlooker than a participant. I get all the pleasures of diversion and excitement, and none of the stress of risk and discipline. But that is not what you want from me, and I know it. Forgive me for looking on, and enable me to enter in, by faith. Amen.

April 21

Take It by Force

"From the days of John the Baptist until now the kingdom of heaven has suffered violence, and the violent take it by force. For all the prophets and the law prophesied until John came; and if you are willing to accept it, he is Elijah who is to come. Let anyone with ears listen!"

Matthew 11:12–15

Intense listening is what is required from us, not religious poll-taking, not theological opinion-sampling. The spiritual danger that we face is casualness, the indifference that treats the word of God on the same level as the newspaper editorial. True faith is energetic and single-minded.

Why is John compared with Elijah?

Your warnings, O God, are frequent and insistent—and necessarily so, for I let things slide, permit junk distractions to divert me from responding to your love and pursuing your will with my whole heart and mind and strength. Develop ardor in me, and keep me centered on you. Amen.

This Generation

"But to what will I compare this generation? It is like children sitting in the marketplaces and calling to one another, 'We played the flute for you, and you did not dance; we wailed, and you did not mourn.' For John came neither eating nor drinking, and they say, 'He has a demon'; the Son of Man came eating and drinking, and they say, 'Look, a glutton and a drunkard, a friend of tax collectors and sinners!' Yet wisdom is vindicated by her deeds."

MATTHEW 11:16–19

Every generation wants God to dance to its tune. And every generation complains that God doesn't meet its expectations—like bored and whining children. But it is God who makes demands on us, not we on him. It is God who includes us in his plans, not we who include him in ours.

What was the difference between John and Jesus?

I pick up the consumer mentality, Lord, and shop for religion the way I shop for groceries—sorting through the shelves (the churches!) to find what suits my taste. Forgive me. Let me be still before you, and respond to all that you are for me, in faith, in adoration. Amen.

April 23

Woe to You!

Then he began to reproach the cities in which most of his deeds of power had been done, because they did not repent. "Woe to you, Chorazin! Woe to you, Bethsaida! For if the deeds of power done in you had been done in Tyre and Sidon, they would have repented long ago in sackcloth and ashes. But I tell you, on the day of judgment it will be more tolerable for Tyre and Sidon than for you. And you, Capernaum, will you be exalted to heaven? No, you will be brought down to Hades. For if the deeds of power done in you had been done in Sodom, it would have remained until this day. But I tell you that on the day of judgment it will be more tolerable for the land of Sodom than for you."

MATTHEW 11:20–24

We can always look around us and find people who are more wicked than we are and feel that we are not so bad after all. We get justification by comparison. But God does not grade on the curve. We are not judged in comparison with others, but by our response to God.

Why is Sodom famous?

Have mercy on me, Christ. I see myself in the mirror of your word and see so much that I have done that is wrong, and so much that I have not done that is essential. I don't want to just get by with the approval of my peers, but to become whole by your grace. Amen.

April 24

Revealed

At that time Jesus said, "I thank you, Father, Lord of heaven and earth, because you have hidden these things from the wise and the intelligent and have revealed them to infants; yes, Father, for such was your gracious will. All things have been handed over to me by my Father; and no one knows the Son except the Father, and no one knows the Father except the Son and anyone to whom the Son chooses to reveal him."

MATTHEW 11:25–27

God shows himself; he does not hide himself. God delights in letting us in on his plans and actions; he does not tease us with coquettish hints. There is mystery in the gospel, true, but it is the mystery of light, not darkness, or more reality than we can take in, not arcane secrets withheld from us.

What is the most important truth revealed to you?

I am full of praise, Lord God, for all that you show me, for everything that you reveal to me. I thank you for including me in what you are doing so that I can participate intelligently, for telling me what you are doing so that I can live in the light and not stumble in the dark. Amen.

April 25

Come to Me

"Come to me, all you that are weary and are carrying heavy burdens, and I will give you rest. Take my yoke upon you, and learn from me; for I am gentle and humble in heart, and you will find rest for your souls. For my yoke is easy, and my burden is light."

MATTHEW 11:28–30

The day teems with possibilities. Jesus's command rouses us out of a sleepy timidity. He doesn't tell us to go out into the world and conquer it; he calls us into a yoked companionship with himself. He doesn't ask us to do anything that he doesn't promise to do with us. We are not so much sent out as invited along.

How does Jesus's yoke work in your life?

"Come unto Me, ye weary, and I will give you rest. O Blessed voice of Jesus, which comes to hearts oppressed! It tells of benediction, of pardon, grace, and peace, of joy that hath no ending, of love which cannot cease." * Amen.

---

* William C. Dix, "Come unto Me, Ye Weary," *The Hymnbook*, 233.

April 26

Lord of the Sabbath

At that time Jesus went through the grainfields on the sabbath; his disciples were hungry, and they began to pluck heads of grain and to eat. When the Pharisees saw it, they said to him, "Look, your disciples are doing what is not lawful to do on the sabbath." He said to them, "Have you not read what David did when he and his companions were hungry? He entered the house of God and ate the bread of the Presence, which it was not lawful for him or his companions to eat, but only for the priests. Or have you not read in the law that on the sabbath the priests in the temple break the sabbath and yet are guiltless? I tell you, something greater than the temple is here. But if you had known what this means, 'I desire mercy and not sacrifice,' you would not have condemned the guiltless. For the Son of Man is lord of the sabbath."

MATTHEW 12:1–8

Jesus concentrates on the personal. He cuts through the maze of regulations and customs that we accumulate and elaborate, and discovers the essential act, the core truth. Jesus is full of refreshing common sense.

Review 1 Samuel 21:1–6 as background.

Father, so many things—ideas, customs, concerns—intrude themselves into my life and separate me from devotion to you. Put all these things in their place so that I can be in my proper place, worshiping you and living in love in the world. Amen.

April 27

. . . How to Destroy Him

He left that place and entered their synagogue; a man was there with a withered hand, and they asked him, "Is it lawful to cure on the sabbath?" so that they might accuse him. He said to them, "Suppose one of you has only one sheep and it falls into a pit on the sabbath; will you not lay hold of it and lift it out? How much more valuable is a human being than a sheep! So it is lawful to do good on the sabbath." Then he said to the man, "Stretch out your hand." He stretched it out, and it was restored, as sound as the other. But the Pharisees went out and conspired against him, how to destroy him.

MATTHEW 12:9–14

Jonathan Swift once remarked, "Most of us have just enough religion to make us hate, but not enough to make us love." Here is an instance of it, people hating Jesus. The list of crimes planned and committed on behalf of the deity stretches into a long list.

Why were they plotting? Did they hate Jesus?

Like so many others, God, I want your stamp of approval on what I find comfortable, not a life of repentance and risky faith. Keep watch over my heart today. Quickly expose any scheming that masks itself as "religious concern," but has as its actual purpose the murderous removal of the Redeemer. Amen.

April 28

It Is Only by Beelzebul

When Jesus became aware of this, he departed. Many crowds followed him, and he cured all of them, and he ordered them not to make him known. This was to fulfill what had been spoken through the prophet Isaiah: "Here is my servant, whom I have chosen, my beloved, with whom my soul is well pleased. I will put my Spirit upon him, and he will proclaim justice to the Gentiles. He will not wrangle or cry aloud, nor will anyone hear his voice in the streets. He will not break a bruised reed or quench a smoldering wick until he brings justice to victory. And in his name the Gentiles will hope." Then they brought to him a demoniac who was blind and mute; and he cured him, so that the one who had been mute could speak and see. All the crowds were amazed and said, "Can this be the Son of David?" But when the Pharisees heard it, they said, "It is only by Beelzebul, the ruler of the demons, that this fellow casts out the demons." He knew what they were thinking and said to them, "Every kingdom divided against itself is laid waste, and no city or house divided against itself will stand. If Satan casts out Satan, he is divided against himself; how then will his kingdom stand? If I cast out demons by Beelzebul, by whom do your own exorcists cast them out? Therefore they will be your judges. But if it is by the Spirit of God that I cast out demons, then the kingdom of God has come to you. Or how can one enter a strong man's house and plunder his property, without first tying up the strong man? Then indeed the house can be plundered. Whoever is not with me is against me, and whoever does not gather with me scatters. Therefore I tell you, people will be forgiven for every sin and blasphemy, but blasphemy against the Spirit will not be forgiven. Whoever speaks a word against the Son of Man will be forgiven, but whoever speaks against the Holy Spirit will not be forgiven, either in this age or in the age to come."

MATTHEW 12:15–32

People are always ready with an explanation of reality that eliminates God from their lives—anything to avoid dealing with the love of Christ. Our world is full of debunking, cynical explanations that flatten people and events into a sidewalk sameness.

Why is Jesus so vehement in his response?

Almighty God, I don't want to be in that crowd of people who are standing around on the sidelines criticizing and quibbling; I want to be with those disciples who are listening, and believing, and following. Amen.

April 29

Out of the Abundance

"Either make the tree good, and its fruit good; or make the tree bad, and its fruit bad; for the tree is known by its fruit. You brood of vipers! How can you speak good things, when you are evil? For out of the abundance of the heart the mouth speaks. The good person brings good things out of a good treasure, and the evil person brings evil things out of an evil treasure. I tell you, on the day of judgment you will have to give an account for every careless word you utter; for by your words you will be justified, and by your words you will be condemned."

MATTHEW 12:33–37

"But I didn't really mean it." The excuse is familiar, but unacceptable. Every word reveals what is already in the heart. Whatever the heart is full of, whether good or bad, spills out in the words of our mouths.

What do your words reveal about your heart?

Root, O God, my life deeply in your redeeming work so that the words that casually and accidentally come from my mouth will be words of praise and exclamations of trust. Amen.

April 30

The Sign of the Prophet Jonah

Then some of the scribes and Pharisees said to him, "Teacher, we wish to see a sign from you." But he answered them, "An evil and adulterous generation asks for a sign, but no sign will be given to it except the sign of the prophet Jonah. For just as Jonah was three days and three nights in the belly of the sea monster, so for three days and three nights the Son of Man will be in the heart of the earth. The people of Nineveh will rise up at the judgment with this generation and condemn it, because they repented at the proclamation of Jonah, and see, something greater than Jonah is here! The queen of the South will rise up at the judgment with this generation and condemn it, because she came from the ends of the earth to listen to the wisdom of Solomon, and see, something greater than Solomon is here!"

MATTHEW 12:38–42

Evidence of God's presence and action is accumulating all around us in enormous quantities. If we don't see it, it is because we are looking for the wrong things—for marvels and for sensations instead of for grace and resurrection.

What signs are you looking for?

Train my eyes, O God, to see what is to be seen in Christ—new life from the dead, fresh hope from the grave, divine love renewing human emptiness. Amen.

May 1

Worse than the First

"When the unclean spirit has gone out of a person, it wanders through waterless regions looking for a resting place, but it finds none. Then it says, 'I will return to my house from which I came.' When it comes, it finds it empty, swept, and put in order. Then it goes and brings along seven other spirits more evil than itself, and they enter and live there; and the last state of that person is worse than the first. So will it be also with this evil generation."

MATTHEW 12:43–45

The goal of the Christian way is not human purity, but divine fellowship. Our task is not to sweep and beautify the house so that there is not a speck of evil dust to be found, but to invite our Lord to dwell with us and fill the house with the laughter of forgiveness and the conversation of grace.

How do you apply this scripture to your life?

Lord, you know how I am always coming up with a new scheme for self-improvement, and reducing my role in the spiritual life to that of charwoman, scrubbing and dusting and polishing my moral image. What I need is you, your presence. Come into my heart, Lord Jesus! Amen.

May 2

My Mother and My Brothers

While he was still speaking to the crowds, his mother and his brothers were standing outside, wanting to speak to him. Someone told him, "Look, your mother and your brothers are standing outside, wanting to speak to you." But to the one who had told him this, Jesus replied, "Who is my mother, and who are my brothers?" And pointing to his disciples, he said, "Here are my mother and my brothers! For whoever does the will of my Father in heaven is my brother and sister and mother."

MATTHEW 12:46–50

No one is born into an intimate relationship with Christ. We cannot presume on him. But everyone has access to an intimate life with him—a life of mother or brother or sister. No one is left out by accident of birth; everyone is included by an act of faith.

What is your relationship with Christ?

Lord Jesus, thank you for the newfound intimacies of faith—that there is a family in which all are accepted equally, all loved uniquely, and that I am included in the "all." Amen.

Listen!

That same day Jesus went out of the house and sat beside the sea. Such great crowds gathered around him that he got into a boat and sat there, while the whole crowd stood on the beach. And he told them many things in parables, saying: "Listen! A sower went out to sow. And as he sowed, some seeds fell on the path, and the birds came and ate them up. Other seeds fell on rocky ground, where they did not have much soil, and they sprang up quickly, since they had no depth of soil. But when the sun rose, they were scorched; and since they had no root, they withered away. Other seeds fell among thorns, and the thorns grew up and choked them. Other seeds fell on good soil and brought forth grain, some a hundredfold, some sixty, some thirty. Let anyone with ears listen!"

MATTHEW 13:1–9

Matthew, Mark, and Luke agree in making this the first of the parables. Every word God speaks to us is seed. We must not treat it casually, waste any of it in uncommitted enthusiasm, or permit it to be crowded into oblivion by the words of others.

What kind of soil are you?

Keep speaking, dear Christ, and keep me listening. Let your word take deep root in the soil of my life and bring forth a crop of faith and love and hope, a life lived to the praise of your glory. Amen.

May 4

Why . . . in Parables?

Then the disciples came and asked him, "Why do you speak to them in parables?" He answered, "To you it has been given to know the secrets of the kingdom of heaven, but to them it has not been given. . . . The reason I speak to them in parables is that 'seeing they do not perceive, and hearing they do not listen, nor do they understand.' . . . For this people's heart has grown dull, and their ears are hard of hearing, and they have shut their eyes; so that they might not look with their eyes, and listen with their ears, and understand with their heart and turn—and I would heal them.' But blessed are your eyes, for they see, and your ears, for they hear. Truly I tell you, many prophets and righteous people longed to see what you see, but did not see it, and to hear what you hear, but did not hear it."

MATTHEW 13:10–17

The parable is a tool for deciding, not discussing. For those who want to have conversations about God, the parable is opaque. For those who will look and listen and pray, the parable becomes a means for participation in the life of faith.

Why do you like parables?

Thank you, Lord God, for sharing your secrets with me, for speaking in love and listening in kindness. My life is filled with the sights and sounds of the gospel. How privileged I am! How blessed! Amen.

May 5

He Indeed Bears Fruit

"Hear then the parable of the sower. When anyone hears the word of the kingdom and does not understand it, the evil one comes and snatches away what is sown in the heart; this is what was sown on the path. As for what was sown on rocky ground, this is the one who hears the word and immediately receives it with joy; yet such a person has no root, but endures only for a while, and when trouble or persecution arises . . . that person immediately falls away. As for what was sown among thorns, this is the one who hears the word, but the cares of the world and the lure of wealth choke the word, and it yields nothing. But as for what was sown on good soil, this is the one who hears the word and understands it, who indeed bears fruit and yields, in one case a hundredfold, in another sixty, and in another thirty."

MATTHEW 13:18–23

Every aspect of life is given significance by the word that Christ addresses to us. We understand our empty, barren hours as a failure to respond to Christ, and we understand our full, fertile days as a result of Christ's triumphant word working in us.

What part of the parable are you living today?

Father, interpret my life for me by means of these words so that I may understand everything that takes place today in relation to what you have done and are doing and will do. I don't want to evaluate anything in terms of my effort, but only in the light of your intention and love in Jesus Christ. Amen.

May 6

Weeds

He put before them another parable: "The kingdom of heaven may be compared to someone who sowed good seed in his field; but while everybody was asleep, an enemy came and sowed weeds among the wheat, and then went away. So when the plants came up and bore grain, then the weeds appeared as well. And the slaves of the householder came and said to him, 'Master, did you not sow good seed in your field? Where, then, did these weeds come from?' He answered, 'An enemy has done this.' The slaves said to him, 'Then do you want us to go and gather them?' But he replied, 'No; for in gathering the weeds you would uproot the wheat along with them. Let both of them grow together until the harvest; and at harvest time I will tell the reapers, Collect the weeds first and bind them in bundles to be burned, but gather the wheat into my barn.'"

MATTHEW 13:24–30

Jesus shows no panic in the presence of evil. He does not give his seed-word greenhouse protection. He is confident that good seed has vastly better survival strength than weeds.

What weeds are there in your life?

Dear Christ, train me in such trust that I am able to share your poise. No more doomsday gloom when I find a weed in the garden! I want your confident, relaxed case in the face of the opposition. Amen.

May 7

Like a Mustard Seed

He put before them another parable: "The kingdom of heaven is like a mustard seed that someone took and sowed in his field; it is the smallest of all the seeds, but when it has grown it is the greatest of shrubs and becomes a tree, so that the birds of the air come and make nests in its branches." He told them another parable: "The kingdom of heaven is like yeast that a woman took and mixed in with three measures of flour until all of it was leavened."

MATTHEW 13:31–33

Very frequently, our excuse for being irresponsible is the claim that we are insignificant. Jesus's parables of mustard seed and leaven put a stop to that. It is the unnoticed, invisible movements of Christ in us that become the forests and banquets of his kingdom.

What insignificant, invisible obedience can you engage in today?

I keep looking, God, for the dramatic moment when I can engage in a glorious sacrifice for the faith; you keep presenting me with daily opportunities for belief and obedience and hope. Help me to forget my dreams of melodrama, and accept the reality of your kingdom. Amen.

May 8

The End of the Age

His disciples approached him, saying, "Explain to us the parable of the weeds of the field." He answered, "The one who sows the good seed is the Son of Man; the field is the world, and the good seed are the children of the kingdom; the weeds are the children of the evil one, and the enemy who sowed them is the devil; the harvest is the end of the age, and the reapers are angels. Just as the weeds are collected and burned up with fire, so will it be at the end of the age. The Son of Man will send his angels, and they will collect out of his kingdom all causes of sin and all evildoers, and they will throw them into the furnace of fire, where there will be weeping and gnashing of teeth. Then the righteous will shine like the sun in the kingdom of their Father. Let anyone with ears listen!"

MATTHEW 13:36–43

We live in an antihistorical age. Everyone, it seems, has amnesia. We are immersed in "presentness." Both past and future are drained of content. Taught by Jesus, we comprehend the past as our own story and anticipate the future as his promise, and live with sharp-edged gratitude and vivid hope.

What do you hope for?

Too many people around me, Lord, think of the future, when they think of it at all, with dread. Taught by you, I will anticipate it with joy, knowing that your will is done on earth as it is in heaven. Amen.

May 9

All

"The kingdom of heaven is like treasure hidden in a field, which someone found and hid; then in his joy he goes and sells all that he has and buys that field. Again, the kingdom of heaven is like a merchant in search of fine pearls; on finding one pearl of great value, he went and sold all that he had and bought it."

MATTHEW 13:44-46

The two parables have one word in common: "all." There must be no equivocation, no hesitation, no calculation before God's offer of new life. Everything we have is traded in for everything that God has for us.

What, for you, is included in the "all"?

O God, I don't want to bring a bookkeeper's mind to the life of faith, anxiously adding up columns of what I must give, columns of what I might get. I give all, and accept all. Amen.

May 10

Separate the Evil

"Again, the kingdom of heaven is like a net that was thrown into the sea and caught fish of every kind; when it was full, they drew it ashore, sat down, and put the good into baskets but threw out the bad. So it will be at the end of the age. The angels will come out and separate the evil from the righteous and throw them into the furnace of fire, where there will be weeping and gnashing of teeth.

MATTHEW 13:47–50

Grading, judging, deciding on relative merits—all that is very much a part of the world's life. But we are not good at it—nobody is good at it. Leave it to the angels. The parable emphasizes the reality of judgment, at the same time that it says we have no part in doing it.

Whom are you tempted to judge?

I know, Father, that you are the judge of all the earth, and that you will execute your judgment both firmly and mercifully. I leave all that to you as I throw myself into the work of believing you and loving my neighbors. Amen.

May 11

Trained for the Kingdom

"Have you understood all this?" They answered, "Yes." And he said to them, "Therefore every scribe who has been trained for the kingdom of heaven is like the master of a household who brings out of his treasure what is new and what is old." When Jesus had finished these parables, he left that place.

MATTHEW 13:51–53

The mixture of old and new is what Jesus does so well, and teaches us to do. The gospel does not specialize in either ancient history or modern problems, but rather develops the skills to appropriate diverse treasures of the kingdom for redemption goals.

How does God train you?

What a rich heritage of truth and experience you have given me, God. And what fresh and creative materials you hand me day by day in situations and people. Daily train me in the skills that will make me a good disciple. Amen.

May 12

Except in Their Own Country

He came to his hometown and began to teach the people in their synagogue, so that they were astounded and said, "Where did this man
get this wisdom and these deeds of power? Is not this the carpenter's
son? Is not his mother called Mary? And are not his brothers James
and Joseph and Simon and Judas? And are not all his sisters with us?
Where then did this man get all this?" And they took offense at him.
But Jesus said to them, "Prophets are not without honor except in
their own country and in their own house." And he did not do many
deeds of power there, because of their unbelief.

Matthew 13:54–58

We do it too. We domesticate Jesus. We think we know all about
him, and precisely what he can do and cannot do. We label him
and define him. Our sophomoric knowledge becomes a substitute
for a faith in him.

Does familiarity with Jesus breed contempt?

*Lord Jesus, don't let my minuscule knowledge of your humanity detract
from the enormous mystery of your divinity. Keep me open in faith to the
majesty and glory of your being, and responsive to your power to change
and save. Amen.*

The Five Loaves and the Two Fish

At that time Herod the ruler heard reports about Jesus; and he said to his servants, "This is John the Baptist; he has been raised from the dead, and for this reason these powers are at work in him." For Herod had arrested John, bound him, and put him in prison on account of Herodias, his brother Philip's wife, because John had been telling him, "It is not lawful for you to have her." Though Herod wanted to put him to death, he feared the crowd, because they regarded him as a prophet. But when Herod's birthday came, the daughter of Herodias danced before the company, and she pleased Herod so much that he promised on oath to grant her whatever she might ask. Prompted by her mother, she said, "Give me the head of John the Baptist here on a platter." The king was grieved, yet out of regard for his oaths and for the guests, he commanded it to be given; he sent and had John beheaded in the prison. The head was brought on a platter and given to the girl, who brought it to her mother. His disciples came and took the body and buried it; then they went and told Jesus. Now when Jesus heard this, he withdrew from there in a boat to a deserted place by himself. But when the crowds heard it, they followed him on foot from the towns. When he went ashore, he saw a great crowd; and he had compassion for them and cured their sick. When it was evening, the disciples came to him and said, "This is a deserted place, and the hour is now late; send the crowds away so that they may go into the villages and buy food for themselves." Jesus said to them, "They need not go away; you give them something to eat." They replied, "We have nothing here but five loaves and two fish." And he said, "Bring them here to me." Then he ordered the crowds to sit down on the grass. Taking the five loaves and the two fish, he looked up to heaven, and blessed and broke the loaves, and gave them to the disciples, and the disciples gave them to the crowds. And all ate and were filled; and they took up what was left over of the broken pieces, twelve baskets full. And those who ate were about five thousand men, besides women and children.

MATTHEW 14:1–21

A hillside of hungry families is changed into a well-fed congregation by Jesus's fourfold action: he took, he blessed, he broke, he gave. Those four acts continue to be reenacted, and our poverty transformed into affluence wherever people gather in Christ's name.

How is this miracle continued into your life?

When I examine my own resources, O Christ, I never seem to have enough. When I worship you, I never seem to run out of blessing. Thank you for your abundance, for your never-diminishing power to meet my needs and complete my joy. Amen.

May 14

Take Heart

Immediately he made the disciples get into the boat and go on ahead to the other side, while he dismissed the crowds. And after he had dismissed the crowds, he went up the mountain by himself to pray. When evening came, he was there alone but by this time the boat, battered by the waves, was far from the land, for the wind was against them. And early in the morning he came walking toward them on the sea. But when the disciples saw him walking on the sea, they were terrified, saying, "It is a ghost!" And they cried out in fear. But immediately Jesus spoke to them and said, "Take heart, it is I; do not be afraid."

MATTHEW 14:22–27

While the disciples had been struggling in the boat, Jesus had been praying on the mountain. Their work was getting them nowhere; Jesus, strong from his hours of prayer, gives them what they need.

What is one of the most frightening times of your life?

Thank you for your prayers, Lord Jesus: for bringing God to me, for bringing love to me, for invading my terror with your courage, for saving me. Amen.

Lord, Save Me

Peter answered him, "Lord, if it is you, command me to come to you on the water." He said, "Come." So Peter got out of the boat, started walking on the water, and came toward Jesus. But when he noticed the strong wind, he became frightened, and beginning to sink, he cried out, "Lord, save me!" Jesus immediately reached out his hand and caught him, saying to him, "You of little faith, why did you doubt?" When they got into the boat, the wind ceased. And those in the boat worshiped him, saying, "Truly you are the Son of God."

MATTHEW 14:28–33

Peter moves from brash, untutored enthusiasm, to disabling doubt, to reverent worship. We, like Peter, have to be rescued from the excesses of presumption and saved from the disabling doubt. Worship, not walking on water, is what we are created for.

In what ways are you like Peter?

So many times, God, I venture into things that are over my head, and instead of looking to you to command and direct I look at the impossible odds and the overwhelming difficulties and sink dangerously. "Lord, save me!" Amen.

May 16

Only Touch the Fringe

When they had crossed over, they came to land at Gennesaret. After the people of that place recognized him, they sent word throughout the region and brought all who were sick to him, and begged him that they might touch even the fringe of his cloak; and all who touched it were healed.

MATTHEW 14:34–36

The terrible loneliness of the ill is shown in their desire to touch Jesus. His willingness to be touched, to be intimate with people in need, shows that he shares his complete person, his body as his spirit, with those who crave contact with wholeness.

What do you need from God?

I reach out to you, Savior Christ, hardly knowing what I need much of the time, but knowing that I need you. And you are there, ready to change my emptiness into wholeness. Thank you for your love and compassion. Amen.

Tradition of the Elders

Then Pharisees and scribes came to Jesus from Jerusalem and said, "Why do your disciples break the tradition of the elders? For they do not wash their hands before they eat." He answered them, "And why do you break the commandment of God for the sake of your tradition? For God said, 'Honor your father and your mother,' and, 'Whoever speaks evil of father or mother must surely die.' But you say that whoever tells father or mother, 'Whatever support you might have had from me is given to God,' then that person need not honor the father. So, for the sake of your tradition, you make void the word of God. You hypocrites! Isaiah prophesied rightly about you when he said: 'This people honors me with their lips, but their hearts are far from me; in vain do they worship me, teaching human precepts as doctrines.'" Then he called the crowd to him and said to them, "Listen and understand: it is not what goes into the mouth that defiles a person, but it is what comes out of the mouth that defiles." Then the disciples approached and said to him, "Do you know that the Pharisees took offense when they heard what you said?" He answered, "Every plant that my heavenly Father has not planted will be uprooted. Let them alone; they are blind guides of the blind. And if one blind person guides another, both will fall into a pit."

MATTHEW 15:1–14

Traditions are useful. They are useful the way bark on a tree is useful, to protect the life within. They preserve truth, but they are not truth: all truth must be lived firsthand, from the inner life.

Why are traditions dangerous?

O God, let me never suppose that because I have inherited a few traditions, I therefore have the living truth. Keep me in touch with the immediate acts of faith that respond to your living word in Christ, so that I am resilient and growing in grace, not stiff and fixed in old ways. Amen.

May 18

Explain the Parable

But Peter said to him, "Explain this parable to us." Then he said, "Are you also still without understanding? Do you not see that whatever goes into the mouth enters the stomach, and goes out into the sewer? But what comes out of the mouth proceeds from the heart, and this is what defiles. For out of the heart come evil intentions, murder, adultery, fornication, theft, false witness, slander. These are what defile a person, but to eat with unwashed hands does not defile."

MATTHEW 15:15–20

We are always turning religion into something that we can control and use to demonstrate that we are all right: a system of rules, an arrangement of traditions. Jesus is always probing to the heart, showing us that our disposition, our faith, and our thoughts are at the center of our relationship with God.

What traditions do you have that are worthless?

Forgive me, merciful Christ, for trying to hide behind conventional morality when I should be opening up myself to you for deep and eternal healing. Examine my inner thoughts and create the kind of life in me that will live to the praise of your glory. Amen.

May 19

Have Mercy on Me!

A Canaanite woman . . . came out and started shouting, "Have mercy on me, Lord, Son of David; my daughter is tormented by a demon." But he did not answer her at all. And his disciples came and urged him, saying, "Send her away, for she keeps shouting after us." He answered, "I was sent only to the lost sheep of the house of Israel." But she came and knelt before him, saying, "Lord, help me." He answered, "It is not fair to take the children's food and throw it to the dogs." She said, "Yes, Lord, yet even the dogs eat the crumbs that fall from their masters' table." Then Jesus answered her, "Woman, great is your faith! Let it be done for you as you wish." And her daughter was healed instantly.

MATTHEW 15:22–28

The Canaanite woman with her bold simplicity, absolute lack of guile, and persistent directness teaches us how to ask Christ for what we need. Too often we elaborately and piously negotiate, rather than simply throwing ourselves on the mercy of our Lord.

How do you feel about the disciples in this story?

"Almighty God, who seest that we have no power of ourselves to help ourselves; keep us both outwardly in our bodies, and inwardly in our souls; that we may be defended from all adversities which may happen to the body, and from all evil thoughts which may assault and hurt the soul; through Jesus Christ our Lord. Amen." *

* Book of Common Prayer.

May 20

Bread Enough in the Desert

Then Jesus called his disciples to him and said, "I have compassion for the crowd, because they have been with me now for three days and have nothing to eat; and I do not want to send them away hungry, for they might faint on the way." The disciples said to him, "Where are we to get enough bread in the desert to feed so great a crowd?" Jesus asked them, "How many loaves have you?" They said, "Seven, and a few small fish." Then ordering the crowd to sit down on the ground he took the seven loaves and the fish; and after giving thanks he broke them and gave them to the disciples, and the disciples gave them to the crowds. And all of them ate and were filled; and they took up the broken pieces left over, seven baskets full. Those who had eaten were four thousand men, besides women and children.

Matthew 15:32–38

The meal is one of Jesus's favorite places for ministry. Here a quite ordinary picnic becomes, under Jesus's words and acts, a messianic banquet. The needs that food meets in our bodies, Christ meets in our lives.

Compare this with the earlier meal in Matthew 14:13–21.

Never permit me, Lord, to sit down to a meal without being at least dimly aware of your great precedent-setting actions, whereby inadequately provided food becomes, because you are present, abundantly experienced fullness. Amen.

The Yeast of the Pharisees

The Pharisees and Sadducees came, and to test Jesus they asked him to show them a sign from heaven. He answered them, "When it is evening, you say, 'It will be fair weather, for the sky is red.' And in the morning, 'It will be stormy today, for the sky is red and threatening.' You know how to interpret the appearance of the sky, but you cannot interpret the signs of the times. An evil and adulterous generation asks for a sign, but no sign will be given to it except the sign of Jonah." Then he left them and went away. When the disciples reached the other side, they had forgotten to bring any bread. Jesus said to them, "Watch out, and beware of the yeast of the Pharisees and Sadducees." They said to one another, "It is because we have brought no bread." And becoming aware of it, Jesus said, "You of little faith, why are you talking about having no bread? Do you still not perceive? Do you not remember the five loaves for the five thousand, and how many baskets you gathered? Or the seven loaves for the four thousand, and how many baskets you gathered? How could you fail to perceive that I was not speaking about bread? Beware of the yeast of the Pharisees and Sadducees!" Then they understood that he had not told them to beware of the yeast of bread, but of the teaching of the Pharisees and Sadducees.

MATTHEW 16:1–12

The Pharisees want a Jesus who will dazzle and delight them with signs and miracles; Jesus is only interested in sharing the life of God that will change them into being people of faith who praise.

What are you interested in?

Will I ever, dear Jesus, get over the immature fantasies that dream of great signs and wonders? As if there were not enough of them provided already in both creation and salvation! Purge me from the leaven of sign-seeking so that I may live by faith and in adoration. Amen.

May 22

You Are the Messiah

Now when Jesus came into the district of Caesarea Philippi, he asked his disciples, "Who do people say that the Son of Man is?" And they said, "Some say John the Baptist, but others Elijah, and still others Jeremiah or one of the prophets." He said to them, "But who do you say that I am?" Simon Peter answered, "You are the Messiah, the Son of the living God." And Jesus answered him, "Blessed are you, Simon son of Jonah! For flesh and blood has not revealed this to you, but my Father in heaven. And I tell you, you are Peter, and on this rock I will build my church, and the gates of Hades will not prevail against it. I will give you the keys of the kingdom of heaven, and whatever you bind on earth will be bound in heaven, and whatever you loose on earth will be loosed in heaven."

MATTHEW 16:13–19

At the same time that Peter realizes and confesses that Jesus is the Christ, the one who reveals God to us, Jesus names Peter as the rock on which the church will be built. The moment that we make Christ our Lord, Christ makes us his foundation stones for the building of his living temple in the world.

Have you confessed that Jesus is your Lord and Savior?

Be Lord and Savior to me, dear Jesus. I receive your presence as God's presence; I believe your words as God's words to me; make me what you will, use me how you will. No longer my will but yours be done. Amen.

May 23

If Any Man Would Come . . .

From that time on, Jesus began to show his disciples that he must go to Jerusalem and undergo great suffering at the hands of the elders and chief priests and scribes, and be killed, and on the third day be raised. And Peter took him aside and began to rebuke him, saying, "God forbid it, Lord! This must never happen to you." But he turned and said to Peter, "Get behind me, Satan! You are a stumbling block to me; for you are setting your mind not on divine things but on human things." Then Jesus told his disciples, "If any want to become my followers, let them deny themselves and take up their cross and follow me. For those who want to save their life will lose it, and those who lose their life for my sake will find it. For what will it profit them if they gain the whole world but forfeit their life?"

MATTHEW 16:21–26

We want to follow Jesus, but like Peter we also want to tell Jesus where to go. Jesus doesn't need our advice; he needs our faithful obedience. Discipleship means learning how to listen to Christ, not getting him to listen to us.

What are the supreme conditions for discipleship?

"Jesus calls us: by Thy mercies, Saviour, may we hear Thy call, give our hearts to Thine obedience, serve and love Thee best of all." Amen.

* Cecil Frances Alexander, "Jesus Calls Us," *The Hymnbook*, 234.

May 24

Transfigured Before Them

Six days later, Jesus took with him Peter and James and his brother John and led them up a high mountain, by themselves. And he was transfigured before them, and his face shone like the sun, and his clothes became dazzling white. Suddenly there appeared to them Moses and Elijah, talking with him. Then Peter said to Jesus, "Lord, it is good for us to be here; if you wish, I will make three dwellings here, one for you, one for Moses, and one for Elijah." While he was still speaking, suddenly a bright cloud overshadowed them, and from the cloud a voice said, "This is my Son, the Beloved; with him I am well pleased; listen to him!" When the disciples heard this, they fell to the ground and were overcome by fear. But Jesus came and touched them, saying, "Get up and do not be afraid." And when they looked up, they saw no one except Jesus himself alone.

MATTHEW 17:1–8

Because he makes himself so accessible to us, we are in constant danger of reducing Jesus to a hail-fellow-well-met. But there is a terrifying majesty in him that occasionally becomes apparent to us. When it does it is unthinkable that we should treat him as a cosmic buddy-we can only fall down in awe and worship.

What do you think of Peter's proposal?

Lord Jesus Christ, open my eyes to the reality of your glory, to the splendor of your loveliness. I worship you. I praise you. I center my life in you, and only you. Amen.

Tell No One About the Vision

As they were coming down the mountain, Jesus ordered them, "Tell no one about the vision until after the Son of Man has been raised from the dead." And the disciples asked him, "Why, then, do the scribes say that Elijah must come first?" He replied, "Elijah is indeed coming and will restore all things; but I tell you that Elijah has already come, and they did not recognize him, but they did to him whatever they pleased. So also the Son of Man is about to suffer at their hands." Then the disciples understood that he was speaking to them about John the Baptist.

MATTHEW 17:9–13

Visions are not for telling. They are too easily turned into gossip—sensational stuff for entertaining dull lives. And they are not to be used for advertising in a world greedy for the latest novelty. Visions are for faith—to put a cosmic scaffolding around the passion.

How was John the Baptist like Elijah?

Thank you, O God, for showing me the essential identity of the Transfigured Christ and the Crucified Christ, the Christ who is one with me in suffering. Amen.

May 26

Faith as a Grain

When they came to the crowd, a man came to him, knelt before him, and said, "Lord, have mercy on my son, for he is an epileptic and he suffers terribly; he often falls into the fire and often into the water. And I brought him to your disciples, but they could not cure him." Jesus answered, "You faithless and perverse generation, how much longer must I be with you? How much longer must I put up with you? Bring him here to me." And Jesus rebuked the demon and it came out of him, and the boy was cured instantly. Then the disciples came to Jesus privately and said, "Why could we not cast it out?" He said to them, "Because of your little faith. For truly I tell you, if you have faith the size of a mustard seed, you will say to this mountain, 'Move from here to there,' and it will move."

MATTHEW 17:14–21

The world's program is self-improvement: resolutions and calisthenics. Jesus's program is faith and prayers: believing and praising. We fail in the work of grace and love when there is too much of us and not enough of God.

What do you find yourself unable to do?

What I usually do, God, when I find that I am inadequate for a task, is to find some way to become more adequate; and you seem to be telling me that what I need to do is to deepen my dependence on you. Amen.

May 27

Then the Children Are Free

When they reached Capernaum, the collectors of the temple tax came to Peter and said, "Does your teacher not pay the temple tax?" He said, "Yes, he does." And when he came home, Jesus spoke of it first, asking, "What do you think, Simon? From whom do kings of the earth take toll or tribute? From their children or from others?" When Peter said, "From others," Jesus said to him, "Then the children are free. However, so that we do not give offense to them, go to the sea and cast a hook; take the first fish that comes up; and when you open its mouth, you will find a coin; take that and give it to them for you and me."

MATTHEW 17:24–27

The freedom of the Christian is not tied to economics or politics or a judicial system. It comes from a relationship between Father and son (and daughter). It is not achieved by human violence, but is the quiet result of divine grace.

Compare this with Galatians 5:1.

Instead of demanding the freedom that I don't have, show me how to discover and enjoy the freedom that I do have—the freedom that flows from being in relationship with you, Father, and which releases me to a life of service and praise. Amen.

May 28

Become Like Children

At that time the disciples came to Jesus and asked, "Who is the greatest in the kingdom of heaven?" He called a child, whom he put among them, and said, "Truly I tell you, unless you change and become like children, you will never enter the kingdom of heaven. Whoever becomes humble like this child is the greatest in the kingdom of heaven. Whoever welcomes one such child in my name welcomes me. If any of you put a stumbling block before one of these little ones who believe in me, it would be better for you if a great millstone were fastened around your neck and you were drowned in the depth of the sea."

MATTHEW 18:1–6

Jesus is not asking us to do anything that he did not do himself: he entered our humanity in the form of infancy. All his commands and counsel were first lived out in his own life. As children before the Father, we live in expectant awe and joyous trust.

What is characteristic of children?

Return me, gracious Christ, to the basic realities of life that are conspicuous in children, but obscure and unattended in adulthood: an eagerness to believe, a readiness to receive, a willingness to love and be loved. Amen.

May 29

Cut It Off

Woe to the world because of stumbling blocks! Occasions for stumbling are bound to come, but woe to the one by whom the stumbling block comes!

If your hand or your foot causes you to stumble, cut it off and throw it away; it is better for you to enter life maimed or lame than to have two hands or two feet and to be thrown into the eternal fire.

And if your eye causes you to stumble, tear it out and throw it away; it is better for you to enter life with one eye than to have two eyes and to be thrown into the hell of fire.

MATTHEW 18:7–9

Jesus is ruthlessly intolerant of any word or act that delays or diverts us from entering into life. These are fierce words: only understandable when we realize that nothing less than everything—eternal life—is at stake.

What interferes with your life of faith?

Save me, Lord, from the world's lazy tolerance, which masks uncertain commitments and failed visions. Sharpen my instincts for survival so that I am alert to repudiate anything that would interfere with my relationship with you. Amen.

May 30

One of These Little Ones

"Take care that you do not despise one of these little ones; for, I tell you, in heaven their angels continually see the face of my Father in heaven. What do you think? If a shepherd has a hundred sheep, and one of them has gone astray, does he not leave the ninety-nine on the mountains and go in search of the one that went astray? And if he finds it, truly I tell you, he rejoices over it more than over the ninety-nine that never went astray. So it is not the will of your Father in heaven that one of these little ones should be lost."

MATTHEW 18:10–13

God is not interested in percentages-even an overwhelming 99 percent is unsatisfactory to him. He wants everyone. He doesn't write off anybody. And that should keep us from ignoring or despising or forgetting anyone, even the least. Especially the least!

Who are the "little ones" in your life?

Forgive me, O God, for slighting people who are on the fringes of society and seeking out the people who are important and influential. Give me the shepherd's heart, always on the lookout for the lost and the hurt, after the manner of Jesus. Amen.

May 31

Two or Three

"If another member of the church sins against you, go and point out the fault when the two of you are alone. If the member listens to you, you have regained that one. But if you are not listened to, take one or two others along with you, so that every word may be confirmed by the evidence of two or three witnesses. If the member refuses to listen to them, tell it to the church; and if the offender refuses to listen even to the church, let such a one be to you as a Gentile and a tax collector. Truly I tell you, whatever you bind on earth will be bound in heaven, and whatever you loose on earth will be loosed in heaven. Again, truly I tell you, if two of you agree on earth about anything you ask, it will be done for you by my Father in heaven. For where two or three are gathered in my name, I am there among them."

MATTHEW 18:15–20

We would get on better if we could ignore or dismiss offending people. A private religion would be much more to our taste. But God will not permit it: we must learn God's forgiveness and love among people whom we forgive and love.

Who has sinned against you?

Give me the courage, Lord Jesus, to face the people today who have displeased or hurt or troubled me. Help me to forgive them, not condemn them. By your grace draw me into a community with them where together we experience your presence. Amen.

June 1

How Often?

Then Peter came and said to him, "Lord, if another member of the church sins against me, how often should I forgive? As many as seven times?" Jesus said to him, "Not seven times, but, I tell you, seventy-seven times. For this reason the kingdom of heaven may be compared to a king who wished to settle accounts with his slaves. When he began the reckoning, one who owed him ten thousand talents was brought to him; and, as he could not pay, his lord ordered him to be sold, together with his wife and children and all his possessions, and payment to be made. So the slave fell on his knees before him, saying, 'Have patience with me, and I will pay you everything.' And out of pity for him, the lord of that slave released him and forgave him the debt. But that same slave, as he went out, came upon one of his fellow slaves who owed him a hundred denarii; and seizing him by the throat, he said, 'Pay what you owe.' Then his fellow slave fell down and pleaded with him, 'Have patience with me, and I will pay you.' But he refused; then he went and threw him into prison until he would pay the debt. When his fellow slaves saw what had happened, they were greatly distressed, and they went and reported to their lord all that had taken place. Then his lord summoned him and said to him, 'You wicked slave! I forgave you all that debt because you pleaded with me. Should you not have had mercy on your fellow slave, as I had mercy on you?' And in anger his lord handed him over to be tortured until he would pay his entire debt. So my heavenly Father will also do to every one of you, if you do not forgive your brother or sister from your heart."

MATTHEW 18:21–35

Peter asked for a statistical count; Jesus gave him a story. We do not calculate forgiveness by numbers; we live it out in a world of incalculable mercy.

Whom do you need to forgive?

Your stories, Jesus, describe a world I can't really see, a world large with generosity. Every mean act and every failed task is released from condemnation. I want to share in this world, Lord, of forgiving and being forgiven. Amen.

June 2

Is It Lawful?

Some Pharisees came to Jesus, and to test him they asked, "Is it lawful for a man to divorce his wife for any cause?" He answered, "Have you not read that the one who made them at the beginning 'made them male and female,' and said, 'For this reason a man shall leave his father and mother and be joined to his wife, and the two shall become one flesh'? So they are no longer two, but one flesh. Therefore what God has joined together, let no one separate." They said to him, "Why then did Moses command us to give a certificate of dismissal and to divorce her?" He said to them, ". . . I say to you, whoever divorces his wife, except for unchastity, and marries another commits adultery."

MATTHEW 19:3–9

Some people come to Jesus and say, "Help me; have mercy upon me." Jesus responds immediately and graciously. Others, like these Pharisees, come and say, "Is it lawful...?" They are interested not in what God can do for them, but in what they can get by with. All they get from Jesus is some quotations from Genesis.

What scripture does Jesus quote?

Now, Father, I see why some of my prayers are unsatisfactory: I am interested in my possibilities rather than in your grace. I ask for information rather than for mercy. I see the difference; now help me to pray the difference. Amen.

161

June 3

To Whom It Is Given

His disciples said to him, "If such is the case of a man with his wife, it is better not to marry." But he said to them, "Not everyone can accept this teaching, but only those to whom it is given. For there are eunuchs who have been so from birth, and there are eunuchs who have been made eunuchs by others, and there are eunuchs who have made themselves eunuchs for the sake of the kingdom of heaven. Let anyone accept this who can."

MATTHEW 19:10–12

Jesus doesn't impose a uniform way of life on everyone. There are different ways of life in which to pursue a committed discipleship. God gives the means to accomplish the ends that he commands in us.

In what station in life has God placed you?

Create a contentment in me, God, with the circumstances of my life. It is so inwardly destructive to be always wishing I were in a different situation or involved in other relationships. Show me how to do the best in love and faith right where I am. Amen.

June 4

Lay His Hands on Them and Pray

Then little children were being brought to him in order that he might lay his hands on them and pray. The disciples spoke sternly to those who brought them; but Jesus said, "Let the little children come to me, and do not stop them; for it is to such as these that the kingdom of heaven belongs." And he laid his hands on them and went on his way.

Matthew 19:13–15

The extremities of existence are joined in Jesus's life: he touches children, immersing himself in the sensual, physical realities of the human; and he prays, laying hold of the unseen, spiritual realities of God.

Do you separate the physical and spiritual?

I want to be equally at home, Lord Jesus, in material, physical things and in spiritual, divine realities—in the same way that you were, touching and praying. Amen.

Give to the Poor

Then someone came to him and said, "Teacher, what good deed must I do to have eternal life?" And he said to him, "Why do you ask me about what is good? There is only one who is good. If you wish to enter into life, keep the commandments." He said to him, "Which ones?" And Jesus said, "You shall not murder; You shall not commit adultery; You shall not steal; You shall not bear false witness; Honor your father and mother; also, You shall love your neighbor as yourself." The young man said to him, "I have kept all these; what do I still lack?" Jesus said to him, "If you wish to be perfect, go, sell your possessions, and give the money to the poor, and you will have treasure in heaven; then come, follow me." When the young man heard this word, he went away grieving, for he had many possessions.

MATTHEW 19:16–22

The young man thought that he had kept the Levitical command, "Love your neighbor as yourself," but it had never occurred to him that his neighbor might be the poor man and that love had something to do with how he spent his money.

Who are some of the unseen "neighbors" in your life?

I know the commands, O God, but I need your help in seeing the people and circumstances where my obedience is commanded. Open my hands that have been clutching possessions; open my eyes too long blind to certain neighbors. Amen.

Who Then Can Be Saved?

Then Jesus said to his disciples, "Truly I tell you, it will be hard for a rich person to enter the kingdom of heaven. Again I tell you, it is easier for a camel to go through the eye of a needle than for someone who is rich to enter the kingdom of God." When the disciples heard this, they were greatly astounded and said, "Then who can be saved?" But Jesus looked at them and said, "For mortals it is impossible, but for God all things are possible." Then Peter said in reply, "Look, we have left everything and followed you. What then will we have?" Jesus said to them, "Truly I tell you, at the renewal of all things, when the Son of Man is seated on the throne of his glory, you who have followed me will also sit on twelve thrones, judging the twelve tribes of Israel. And everyone who has left houses or brothers or sisters or father or mother or children or fields, for my name's sake, will receive a hundredfold."

MATTHEW 19:23–29

We have to make a choice between possessing as much as we can manage, proving we are worth something by our visible wealth, and traveling light in faith, believing that we are worth everything simply because God loves us.

What have you left?

As long, Father, as I harbor covetous desires to be among the first, I am never free to respond quickly and spontaneously to your presence and your word. Forgive me for wanting to be among the rich, and for avoiding the company of the poor, where you are. Amen.

June 7

The Last Will Be First

"For the kingdom of heaven is like a landowner who went out early in the morning to hire laborers for his vineyard. After agreeing with the laborers for the usual daily wage, he sent them into his vineyard. When he went out about nine o'clock, he saw others standing idle in the marketplace; and he said to them, 'You also go into the vineyard, and I will pay you whatever is right.' So they went. When he went out again about noon and about three o'clock, he did the same. And about five o'clock he went out and found others standing around; and he said to them, 'Why are you standing here idle all day?' They said to him, 'Because no one has hired us.' He said to them, 'You also go into the vineyard.' When evening came, the owner of the vineyard said to his manager, 'Call the laborers and give them their pay, beginning with the last and then going to the first.' When those hired about five o'clock came, each of them received the usual daily wage. Now when the first came, they thought they would receive more; but each of them also received the usual daily wage. And when they received it, they grumbled against the landowner, saying, 'These last worked only one hour, and you have made them equal to us who have borne the burden of the day and the scorching heat.' But he replied to one of them, 'Friend, I am doing you no wrong; did you not agree with me for the usual daily wage? Take what belongs to you and go; I choose to give to this last the same as I give to you. Am I not allowed to do what I choose with what belongs to me? Or are you envious because I am generous?' So the last will be first, and the first will be last."

Matthew 20:1–16

Christ doesn't run the world by consulting us, asking what we think is right or proper. Naturally, we make our share of complaints against his administration. But much of our discontent, phrased as a concern for justice, is only petty envy and small-minded jealousy.

What don't you like about how God runs things?

You are right on target, Lord, when you ask me, "Do you begrudge my generosity?" It is not easy to get used to a life of extravagant mercy, when I have grown up on nit-picking calculations of rights and benefits. Amen.

June 8

The Son of Man Will Be Handed Over

While Jesus was going up to Jerusalem, he took the twelve disciples aside by themselves, and said to them on the way, "See, we are going up to Jerusalem, and the Son of Man will be handed over to the chief priests and scribes, and they will condemn him to death; then they will hand him over to the Gentiles to be mocked and flogged and crucified; and on the third day he will be raised."

MATTHEW 20:17–19

Association with Jesus puts us in the company of healing, enlightenment, and unanticipated joys. But it also puts us in the place of betrayal, humiliation, and crucifixion. We must, if we are faithful to the Christian way, accept the one as readily as the other.

Why is this announcement a surprise?

I Will not forget, Lord Christ, when I experience apprehension and dread, that is is an announced and documented part of the life of discipleship. Keep me faithful in the difficult trials as you accompany me with the promise of resurrection. Amen.

June 9

His Life a Ransom for Many

Then the mother of the sons of Zebedee came to him with her sons
. . . , "Declare that these two sons of mine will sit, one at your right
hand and one at your left, in your kingdom." But Jesus answered,
"You do not know what you are asking. Are you able to drink the cup
that I am about to drink?" They said to him, "We are able." He said
to them, "You will indeed drink my cup, but to sit at my right hand
and at my left, this is not mine to grant, but it is for those for whom
it has been prepared by my Father." When the ten heard it, they were
angry with the two brothers. But Jesus called them to him and said,
"You know that the rulers of the Gentiles lord it over them, and their
great ones are tyrants over them. It will not be so among you; but
whoever wishes to be great among you must be your servant, and
whoever wishes to be first among you must be your slave; just as the
Son of Man came not to be served but to serve, and to give his life a
ransom for many."

MATTHEW 20:20–28

We attempt to get the respect and recognition of a life of discipleship by acquiring a few pious habits. Jesus demands a life that
makes a difference: a life of service, a life of giving.

How do you live as a servant?

*My confession, Lord: I keep hoping that being a Christian will give me an
advantage over everybody else; I make a habit of looking for loopholes in
your demands for a life of service. Forgive me, for Jesus's sake. Amen.*

June 10

What Do You Want?

As they were leaving Jericho, a large crowd followed him. There were two blind men sitting by the roadside. When they heard that Jesus was passing by, they shouted, "Lord, have mercy on us, Son of David!" The crowd sternly ordered them to be quiet; but they shouted even more loudly, "Have mercy on us, Lord, Son of David!" Jesus stood still and called them, saying, "What do you want me to do for you?" They said to him, "Lord, let our eyes be opened." Moved with compassion, Jesus touched their eyes. Immediately they regained their sight and followed him.

MATTHEW 20:29–34

The blind men's answer to Jesus's question seems obvious: "Let our eyes be opened." But had they ever asked for that before? Or had they long ago gotten accustomed to asking for handouts? Jesus forces us to what is basic and essential: what do you really want?

What do you want?

Gracious Father, years of living in "Jericho" have turned me into a passive consumer, dependent on alms. My desires and wants are exceedingly trivial. You rouse in me soul-sized thirsts I had forgotten I had: I want sight. I want salvation. Amen.

June 11

Mount of Olives

When they had come near Jerusalem and had reached Bethphage, at the Mount of Olives, Jesus sent two disciples, saying to them, "Go into the village ahead of you, and immediately you will find a donkey tied, and a colt with her; untie them and bring them to me. If anyone says anything to you, just say this, 'The Lord needs them.' And he will send them immediately." This took place to fulfill what had been spoken through the prophet, saying, "Tell the daughter of Zion, Look, your king is coming to you, humble, and mounted on a donkey, and on a colt, the foal of a donkey."

MATTHEW 21:1–5

First-century Jewish expectation had fixed on the Mount of Olives as the site for the appearance of the Messiah. As Jesus prepared to present himself at the Jerusalem Passover, he partially fit into their expectations. At the same time, he confounded them by selecting a plodding beast of burden to ride rather than a dashing war horse.

Look at a map of the Holy Land and visualize the relation of the Mount of Olives to Jerusalem.

I want to be ready, Jesus, for your daily entrance into my life. I know that you will come to me. I also know that the way you will come will differ from my preconceptions. Prepare me to receive you as you will to come. Amen.

June 12

Did as Jesus Directed

The disciples went and did as Jesus had directed them; They brought the donkey and the colt, and put their cloaks on them, and he sat on them.

MATTHEW 21:6–7

Simple obedience is a marvelous act: when we do what Jesus tells us to do, everything falls into place, things work out. Why do we think we have to improve on his commands, edit his instructions?

Are you basically an obeyer or a kibitzer?

Almighty and eternal God, speak your word to my heart, commanding what you will. And then work in me the grace of obedience enabling me in faith to carry out your word. Amen.

June 13

Branches from the Trees

A very large crowd spread their cloaks on the road, and others cut branches from the trees and spread them on the road.

MATTHEW 21:8

Festivity was in the air. Our custom at parades is to wave banners and pompoms; the Hebrews made a red carpet with garments and tree branches. They knew something celebrative was taking place in Jesus and they wanted in on it.

What is celebrative for you in Jesus?

"Joyful, joyful, we adore Thee, God of glory, Lord of love; hearts unfold like flowers before Thee, opening to the sun above. Melt the clouds of sin and sadness, drive the dark of doubt away; giver of immortal gladness, fill us with the light of day." * Amen.

---

* Henry van Dyke, "Joyful, Joyful, We Adore Thee," *The Hymnbook*, 31.

June 14

Hosanna in the Highest!

The crowds that went ahead of him and that followed were shouting, "Hosanna to the Son of David! Blessed is the one who comes in the name of the Lord! Hosanna in the highest heaven!"

MATTHEW 21:9

Hosanna means "Save now!" It is a cry for help in the context of assured response. The Savior has arrived! Salvation is at hand! Everyone's life is at the point of change for the better. That which none of us can do for ourselves is done for us in Jesus.

Read Psalm 118:25–26 for the source of this cry.

"Thou didst accept their praises; accept the prayers we bring, who in all good delightest, Thou good and gracious King! All glory, laud, and honor to Thee, Redeemer, King, to whom the lips of children made sweet hosannas ring!" Amen.

---

* Theodolph of Orleans, "All Glory, Laud, and Honor," *The Hymnbook,* 171.

The Whole City Was in Turmoil

When he entered Jerusalem, the whole city was in turmoil, asking, "Who is this?" The crowds were saying, "This is the prophet Jesus from Nazareth in Galilee."

MATTHEW 21:10–11

Many things are put together in this parade: the obedience of disciples, the generosity of the donkey's owner, the prophecy of Zechariah, the enthusiasm of crowds, the praise of God. The final week of Jesus's ministry opens with a celebration. It will conclude with a resurrection.

What part do you play in celebrating Christ's rule?

God, I want to find my proper place among people who praise you. By your grace every day is a festival of salvation. Put a palm branch in my hand and a song in my mouth as I join the people who know the joyful sound. Amen.

June 16

Den of Robbers

Then Jesus entered the temple and drove out all who were selling and buying in the temple, and he overturned the tables of the money changers and the seats of those who sold doves. He said to them, "It is written, 'My house shall be called a house of prayer'; but you are making it a den of robbers."

MATTHEW 21:12–13

Places of worship are bustling centers of activity: centers for discussion groups, work projects, social gatherings—and, of course, a brief prayer to get things started on the right note. Most churches could stand a good temple-cleaning.

Is prayer the central activity in your church?

When I next enter my church, Father, I will pray. I will not go to talk about you, or talk to my neighbors, but to address you and be addressed by you. Keep me faithful and attentive to the conversation that you are having with me in Jesus Christ. Amen.

June 17

Prepared Praise

The blind and the lame came to him in the temple, and he cured them. But when the chief priests and the scribes saw the amazing things that he did, and heard the children crying out in the temple, "Hosanna to the Son of David," they became angry and said to him, "Do you hear what these are saying?" Jesus said to them, "Yes; have you never read, 'Out of the mouths of infants and nursing babies you have prepared praise for yourself'?" He left them, went out of the city to Bethany, and spent the night there.

MATTHEW 21:14–17

The noise of the money changers never, apparently, had bothered them, but the noise of children was intolerable. How could they become so quickly accustomed to the clangor of commerce, and be so short-tempered with the shouts of children? How can we?

What psalm does Jesus quote?

"Come, Thou Fount of every blessing, tune my heart to sing Thy grace; streams of mercy, never ceasing, call for songs of loudest praise. Teach me some melodious sonnet, sung by flaming tongues above; praise the mount! I'm fixed upon it, mount of God's unchanging love!" * Amen.

* R. Robinson, "Come, Thou Fount of Every Blessing," *The Hymnbook*, 322.

June 18

Whatever You Ask in Prayer

In the morning, when he returned to the city, he was hungry. And seeing a fig tree by the side of the road, he went to it and found nothing at all on it but leaves. Then he said to it, "May no fruit ever come from you again!" And the fig tree withered at once. When the disciples saw it, they were amazed, saying, "How did the fig tree wither at once?" Jesus answered them, "Truly I tell you, if you have faith and do not doubt, not only will you do what has been done to the fig tree, but even if you say to this mountain, 'Be lifted up and thrown into the sea,' it will be done. Whatever you ask for in prayer with faith, you will receive."

MATTHEW 21:18–22

Jesus trains us to seek the essentials from God, to direct our longings and aspirations to the center. Prayer to God must become as common in our lives as conversation with our friends.

Is prayer central in your life?

God and Father, I find your love in and around me; I realize your salvation working deeply through my existence. Centered in you and surrounded by you, make every word I speak a prayer, in the name of Jesus Christ. Amen.

By What Authority?

When he entered the temple, the chief priests and the elders of the people came to him as he was teaching, and said, "By what authority are you doing these things, and who gave you this authority?" Jesus said to them, "I will also ask you one question; if you tell me the answer, then I will also tell you by what authority I do these things. Did the baptism of John come from heaven, or was it of human origin?" And they argued with one another, "If we say, 'From heaven,' he will say to us, 'Why then did you not believe him?' But if we say, 'Of human origin,' we are afraid of the crowd; for all regard John as a prophet." So they answered Jesus, "We do not know." And he said to them, "Neither will I tell you by what authority I am doing these things."

MATTHEW 21:23–27

The question was not an honest request for information, but a tactic for avoiding personal responsibility. They asked questions about Jesus's credentials so that they would not have to answer the question Jesus's life posed to their lives.

Do you ever ask questions to avoid giving answers?

I want my life, Lord, to be an answer to your love for me: my actions and my words, my thoughts and my dreams—all a response to the great reality of your presence in Jesus, that calls into question my selfishness and my pride. Amen.

Which of the Two

"What do you think? A man had two sons; he went to the first and said, 'Son, go and work in the vineyard today.' He answered, 'I will not'; but later he changed his mind and went. The father went to the second and said the same; and he answered, 'I go, sir'; but he did not go. Which of the two did the will of his father?" They said, "The first." Jesus said to them, "Truly I tell you, the tax collectors and the prostitutes are going into the kingdom of God ahead of you." For John came to you in the way of righteousness and you did not believe him, but the tax collectors and the prostitutes believed him; and even after you saw it, you did not change your minds and believe him.

MATTHEW 21:28–32

Our life is formed at the deepest levels not by protest and promises, arguments and resolutions, but by faithful obedience. In the silent depths of the soul, the responses formed finally result—in spite of doubts and denials—in a life pleasing to God.

Which of the two sons are you?

God in Christ: you probe my heart and discover behind the words that I speak the life that I live. Purify and sanctify that inner life so that I may please you and glorify your name. Amen.

June 21

What Will He Do to Those Tenants?

"Listen to another parable. There was a landowner who planted a vineyard, put a fence around it, dug a wine press in it, and built a watchtower. Then he leased it to tenants and went to another country. When the harvest time had come, he sent his slaves to the tenants to collect his produce. But the tenants seized his slaves and beat one, killed another, and stoned another. Again he sent other slaves, more than the first; and they treated them in the same way. Finally he sent his son to them, saying, 'They will respect my son.' But when the tenants saw the son, they said to themselves, 'This is the heir; come, let us kill him and get his inheritance.' So they seized him, threw him out of the vineyard, and killed him. Now when the owner of the vineyard comes, what will he do to those tenants?" They said to him, "He will put those wretches to a miserable death, and lease the vineyard to other tenants who will give him the produce at the harvest time."

MATTHEW 21:33–41

Popular-opinion polls condition us to look for truth in the percentages: whatever most people do or think is the most right. The parable exposes the foolishness of statistics: no matter how many times the tenants reject the truth, the truth remains to judge them.

What majority actions today do you think are wrong?

How faithfully you approach me, Lord Jesus! How persistently you enter my life. Open my eyes to your presence and my heart to your grace so that I will always accept your coming. Amen.

June 22

The Very Stone

Jesus said to them, "Have you never read in the scriptures: 'The stone that the builders rejected has become the cornerstone; this was the Lord's doing, and it is amazing in our eyes'? Therefore I tell you, the kingdom of God will be taken away from you and given to a people that produces the fruits of the kingdom. The one who falls on this stone will be broken to pieces; and it will crush anyone on whom it falls." When the chief priests and the Pharisees heard his parables, they realized that he was speaking about them. They wanted to arrest him, but they feared the crowds, because they regarded him as a prophet.

MATTHEW 21:42–46

All the experts who can't fit God into their thinking, or their living, conclude that there is simply no place for him. But they start in the wrong places: we don't fit God into our lives, he fits us into his. When we begin with him, the "head of the corner," our lives are fit for eternity.

What psalm does Jesus quote?

Too many times, O Christ, I have rejected you because you didn't meet my specifications. Forgive me for my shortsighted arrogance. Forgive me for my small-minded selfishness. Build me into the life you are making. Amen.

They Made Light of It

Once more Jesus spoke to them in parables, saying: "The kingdom of heaven may be compared to a king who gave a wedding banquet for his son. He sent his slaves to call those who had been invited to the wedding banquet, but they would not come. Again he sent other slaves, saying, 'Tell those who have been invited: Look, I have prepared my dinner, my oxen and my fat calves have been slaughtered, and everything is ready; come to the wedding banquet.' But they made light of it and went away, one to his farm, another to his business, while the rest seized his slaves, mistreated them, and killed them. The king was enraged. He sent his troops, destroyed those murderers, and burned their city. Then he said to his slaves, 'The wedding is ready, but those invited were not worthy. Go therefore into the main streets, and invite everyone you find to the wedding banquet.' Those slaves went out into the streets and gathered all whom they found, both good and bad; so the wedding hall was filled with guests. But when the king came in to see the guests, he noticed a man there who was not wearing a wedding robe, and he said to him, 'Friend, how did you get in here without a wedding robe?' And he was speechless. Then the king said to the attendants, 'Bind him hand and foot, and throw him into the outer darkness, where there will be weeping and gnashing of teeth.' For many are called, but few are chosen."

MATTHEW 22:1–14

We are faced with a life-or-death summons. The responses that we make to God in Christ are the stuff of eternity. The parable administers a shock of realization that jars us out of our drifting dilettantism.

What part of the parable speaks to you?

Lord, preserve me from such deficiencies of will and love that will keep me from being counted among the blessed celebrants in your presence. I know that I am among the called; grant that I will also be among the chosen. Amen.

June 24

Whose Likeness?

Then the Pharisees went and plotted to entrap him in what he said. So they sent their disciples to him, along with the Herodians, saying, "Teacher, we know that you are sincere, and teach the way of God in accordance with truth, and show deference to no one; for you do not regard people with partiality. Tell us, then, what you think. Is it lawful to pay taxes to the emperor, or not?" But Jesus, aware of their malice, said, "Why are you putting me to the test, you hypocrites? Show me the coin used for the tax." And they brought him a denarius. Then he said to them, "Whose head is this, and whose title?" They answered, "The emperor's." Then he said to them, "Give therefore to the emperor the things that are the emperor's, and to God the things that are God's." When they heard this, they were amazed; and they left him and went away.

MATTHEW 22:15–22

The question was designed to drive a wedge between the secular and the sacred, between what we owe to God and what we owe to society. But Jesus calls us to live in a world without partitions, to the glory of God, responsible to our nation.

How does this help you live well as a citizen?

I want my life, O God, to be consciously and deliberately lived under your sovereign lordship; but I also want to live responsibly as a citizen, through Jesus Christ. Amen.

In the Resurrection

The same day some Sadducees came to him, saying there is no resurrection; and they asked him a question, saying, "Teacher, Moses said, 'If a man dies childless, his brother shall marry the widow, and raise up children for his brother.' Now there were seven brothers among us; the first married, and died childless, leaving the widow to his brother. The second did the same, so also the third, down to the seventh. Last of all, the woman herself died. In the resurrection, then, whose wife of the seven will she be? For all of them had married her." Jesus answered them, "You are wrong, because you know neither the scriptures nor the power of God. For in the resurrection they neither marry nor are given in marriage, but are like angels in heaven. And as for the resurrection of the dead, have you not read what was said to you by God, 'I am the God of Abraham, the God of Isaac, and the God of Jacob'? He is God not of the dead, but of the living." And when the crowd heard it, they were astounded at his teaching.

MATTHEW 22:23–33

Jesus has little patience with people who love nothing better than a good "religious discussion." He is interested in bringing people new life, bringing them into relationship with a living God.

Why did the Sadducees ask the question?

No empty disputes today, Lord, but empty tombs. I don't want to waste any time in clever arguments, but immerse myself intelligently in the scriptures and respond devoutly to the living God. Amen.

June 26

Asked Him a Question

When the Pharisees heard that he had silenced the Sadducees, they gathered together, and one of them, a lawyer, asked him a question to test him. "Teacher, which commandment in the law is the greatest?" He said to him, "You shall love the Lord your God with all your heart, and with all your soul, and with all your mind. This is the greatest and first commandment. And a second is like it: 'You shall love your neighbor as yourself.' On these two commandments hang all the law and the prophets."

MATTHEW 22:34–40

Most religious questions are not in order to acquire information or wisdom, but frivolous camouflages for indolence. As long as we are asking questions, we don't have to do anything. Jesus's answer put a stop to the questions: his answer confronts us with the basic question of our lives. Will we love, or not?

What scripture does Jesus quote?

What will it be for me today, Lord? asking questions or loving in obedience? I don't need to know more, but I do need to love more. Keep me faithful to your command. Amen.

June 27

Whose Son?

Now while the Pharisees were gathered together, Jesus asked them this question: "What do you think of the Messiah? Whose son is he?" They said to him, "The son of David." He said to them, "How is it then that David by the Spirit calls him Lord, saying, 'The Lord said to my Lord, "Sit at my right hand, until I put your enemies under your feet"'? If David thus calls him Lord, how can he be his son?" No one was able to give him an answer, nor from that day did anyone dare to ask him any more questions.

MATTHEW 22:41–46

Jesus answers the question by asking a question. We do not come to Christ to get answers; we come to have our lives called into question, and find how our lives become an answer to him.

What question does Christ address to you? What is your answer?

"I find, I walk, I love, but O the whole of love is but my answer, Lord to Thee! For Thou wert long beforehand with my soul; always Thou lovedst me" * Amen.

---

* Pilgrim Hymnal.

188

June 28

Do Not Practice

Then Jesus said to the crowds and to his disciples, "The scribes and the Pharisees sit on Moses' seat; therefore, do whatever they teach you and follow it; but do not do as they do, for they do not practice what they teach. They tie up heavy burdens, hard to bear, and lay them on the shoulders of others; but they themselves are unwilling to lift a finger to move them. They do all their deeds to be seen by others; for they make their phylacteries broad and their fringes long. They love to have the place of honor at banquets and the best seats in the synagogues, and to be greeted with respect in the marketplaces, and to have people call them rabbi. But you are not to be called rabbi, for you have one teacher, and you are all students. . . . All who exalt themselves will be humbled, and all who humble themselves will be exalted."

MATTHEW 23:1–12

Most people do not start out to be hypocrites. We begin sincerely enough, with good intentions. But as it becomes easier to talk about God than engaging in the arduous process of deepening and growing in faith, we take the easier road. Outside fluency and expertise covers up inner sloth and emptiness.

Are you the same inside as outside?

God, especially when people look to me as some kind of authority on religion, I find it easy to take on the role, meeting their expectations, but ignoring yours. But I want my life to be an on-the-knees response to you, not an on-the-pedestal lording over others. Amen.

June 29

Woe to You

"But woe to you, scribes and Pharisees, hypocrites! For you lock people out of the kingdom of heaven. . . . Woe to you, scribes and Pharisees, hypocrites! For you tithe mint, dill, and cummin, and have neglected the weightier matters of the law: justice and mercy and faith. It is these you ought to have practiced without neglecting the others. You blind guides! You strain out a gnat but swallow a camel! Woe to you, scribes and Pharisees, hypocrites! For you clean the outside of the cup and of the plate, but inside they are full of greed and self-indulgence. You blind Pharisee! First clean the inside of the cup, so that the outside also may become clean. Woe to you, scribes and Pharisees, hypocrites! For you are like whitewashed tombs, which on the outside look beautiful, but inside they are full of the bones of the dead and of all kinds of filth.

MATTHEW 23:13–27

Jesus's anger, verbalized in these lines of indignant thunder, sounds more terrifying after each repetition. The effect is cumulative. The hammering denunciations break up the false front of glib performance and expose the inner emptiness of self-centered smugness.

How many woes are pronounced?

Lord Jesus Christ, I accept the designation "Pharisee" and put myself under your prophetic analysis: expose every tendency in me to separate the inner life of faith and the outer life of reputation; convict me of every instance of saying more than I am living. "Unite my heart to fear thy name" (Psalm 86:11). Amen.

190

June 30

How Often!

"Jerusalem, Jerusalem, the city that kills the prophets and stones those who are sent to it! How often have I desired to gather your children together as a hen gathers her brood under her wings, and you were not willing! See, your house is left to you, desolate. For I tell you, you will not see me again until you say, 'Blessed is the one who comes in the name of the Lord.'"

MATTHEW 23:37–39

The most religious city in history is the site of the worst religious persecution. The place where God showed himself most completely, is the place where God was rejected most vehemently. And the very streets where men and women shouted their hate, Jesus expressed the pathos that would finally convert them to singing hallelujahs.

Who are some of the prophets who were killed and stoned?

Forgive me, O God, for the many times I have rejected your words of invitation, your servants of love. I have not been as loud and public in my rejections as many, but my silent and private unbelief has been, all the same, a refusal. Amen.

July 1

Thrown Down

As Jesus came out of the temple and was going away, his disciples came to point out to him the buildings of the temple. Then he asked them, "You see all these, do you not? Truly I tell you, not one stone will be left here upon another; all will be thrown down."

MATTHEW 24:1–2

The destruction of the temple was spiritual urban renewal—getting rid of an inadequate physical structure so that a "building not made with hands" could be constructed in its place.

What was the purpose of the temple?

God Almighty, I don't want to become so attached to what my ancestors built in obedience to you that I miss the firsthand opportunities of participating in the new things you are doing in my generation. Amen.

July 2

When Will This Be?

When he was sitting on the Mount of Olives, the disciples came to him privately, saying, "Tell us, when will this be, and what will be the sign of your coming and of the end of the age?"

MATTHEW 24:3

The view from where they sat was impressive: Jerusalem panoramic before them, with the magnificent temple in the foreground. But it is not what religious people build that makes the kingdom, but how and when a gracious God comes.

Do you spend most of your time looking at religious sights, or listening to Jesus's words?

Lead me into asking the right questions, Lord God of truth, and train me in a careful listening to your answers. I don't want to stand around looking at the religious scenery; I want to be alert to the new word you are speaking to me in Jesus Christ. Amen.

The End Is Not Yet

Jesus answered them, "Beware that no one leads you astray. For many will come in my name, saying, 'I am the Messiah!' and they will lead many astray. And you will hear of wars and rumors of wars; see that you are not alarmed; for this must take place, but the end is not yet. For nation will rise against nation, and kingdom against kingdom, and there will be famines and earthquakes in various places: all this is but the beginning of the birthpangs."

MATTHEW 24:4–8

A lot of people have franchises these days on predicting the future; it is one of the blue chip businesses in religion. The only thing worse than the crassness of the sellers is the gullibility of the buyers. Jesus warned us well and in detail-there is no excuse for any of us being deceived by these people.

Who has tried to deceive you by pretending to know God's timetable?

It is hard not to be impressed by these people who speak so urgently and convincingly about the future, Jesus—they all claim a direct commission from you. But then I return to these words of warning and their deceit is exposed. I am again content to be obedient at your feet. Amen.

July 4

They Will Hand You Over

"Then they will hand you over to be tortured and will put you to death, and you will be hated by all nations because of my name. Then many will fall away, and they will betray one another and hate one another. And many false prophets will arise and lead many astray. And because of the increase of lawlessness, the love of many will grow cold. But the one who endures to the end will be saved. And this good news of the kingdom will be proclaimed throughout the world, as a testimony to all the nations; and then the end will come."

MATTHEW 24:9–14

If we do not experience betrayal at this moment, we must not therefore become complacent and surprised if and when it comes. Betrayal, which was the fate of Jesus, is also the fate of his followers. Being a Christian is not a surefire way to get ahead in the world.

Have you experienced any of the forms of betrayal mentioned by Jesus?

I don't want my identity as a Christian to be shaped by the culture around me, but by the words that you, Jesus, address to me. How carefully you warned me to keep my guard up against the influencing attitudes of others, whether seductive or hostile. Keep me daily mindful of the dangers. Amen.

If Those Days Had Not Been Cut Short

"So when you see the desolating sacrilege standing in the holy place, as was spoken of by the prophet Daniel (let the reader understand), then those in Judea must flee to the mountains; the one on the house-top must not go down to take what is in the house; the one in the field must not turn back to get a coat. Woe to those who are pregnant and to those who are nursing infants in those days! Pray that your flight may not be in winter or on a sabbath. For at that time there will be great suffering, such as has not been from the beginning of the world until now, no, and never will be. And if those days had not been cut short, no one would be saved; but for the sake of the elect those days will be cut short."

MATTHEW 24:15–22

If history were left to run its course, everybody receiving their moral desserts, the consequences would be merciless and inexorable. But we are not left to our fate; history is interrupted by mercy.

What do you most abhor in current history?

Sovereign and holy Christ: I listen and look at and read the news of the world, and despair—such absurd carnage, such mindless evil. And then I listen and look at and read your salvation and take hope—such mercy, such grace! Amen.

July 6

Do Not Believe It

"Then if anyone says to you, 'Look! Here is the Messiah!' or 'There he
is!'—do not believe it. For false messiahs and false prophets will appear
and produce great signs and omens, to lead astray, if possible, even
the elect. Take note, I have told you beforehand. So, if they say to you,
'Look! He is in the wilderness,' do not go out. If they say, 'Look! He is
in the inner rooms,' do not believe it. For as the lightning comes from
the east and flashes as far as the west, so will be the coming of the Son
of Man. Wherever the corpse is, there the vultures will gather."

MATTHEW 24:23–28

The moment we believe in Jesus Christ as Lord and Savior, we
quit believing a lot of other things. We quit believing in self-
promoting preachers who say they have the latest word from God;
we quit believing in schemes by which we can help ourselves to a
fortune; we quit believing the puffery that puts religious leaders
on pedestals.

Who and what don't you believe in these days?

*You have made things so simple for me, dear Jesus. I simply believe in you.
I don't have to take seriously everyone who speaks seriously in a religious
tone of voice. Thank you for the simplicity of your life, saving me from the
complexities of false Christs and false prophets. Amen.*

Gather His Elect

"Immediately after the suffering of those days the sun will be darkened, and the moon will not give its light; the stars will fall from heaven, and the powers of heaven will be shaken. Then the sign of the Son of Man will appear in heaven, and then all the tribes of the earth will mourn, and they will see 'the Son of Man coming on the clouds of heaven' with power and great glory. And he will send out his angels with a loud trumpet call, and they will gather his elect from the four winds, from one end of heaven to the other."

MATTHEW 24:29–31

The terrible dissolution and falling apart of society and cosmos is decisively countered by the coming of Christ that signals a comprehensive coming together. "Coming together" is the last word, not "falling apart."

What Old Testament scripture is Jesus referring to?

Come, Lord Jesus! Come and save your people, come and save your elect, come and establish your kingdom. Keep me faithful in prayer for your soon coming and aflame in hope. Amen.

July 8

Not Pass Away

"From the fig tree learn its lesson: as soon as its branch becomes tender and puts forth its leaves, you know that summer is near. So also, when you see all these things, you know that he is near, at the very gates. Truly I tell you, this generation will not pass away until all these things have taken place. Heaven and earth will pass away, but my words will not pass away."

MATTHEW 24:32–35

The earth looks so solid, the skies look so immense—and words seem so fragile. But it is the words that will endure, that are full of energy, and that accomplish our redemption, for Christ speaks them.

Reflect on the prominence of "word" in the gospel.

"O God of Light, Thy Word, a lamp unfailing, shines through the darkness of our earthly way, o'er fear and doubt, o'er black despair prevailing, guiding our steps to Thine eternal day." * Amen.

---

* Sarah E. Taylor, "O God of Light, Thy Word, a Lamp Unfailing," *The Hymnbook*, 217.

July 9

You Also Must Be Ready

"But about that day and hour no one knows, neither the angels of heaven, nor the Son, but only the Father. For as the days of Noah were, so will be the coming of the Son of Man. For as in those days before the flood they were eating and drinking, marrying and giving in marriage, until the day Noah entered the ark, and they knew nothing until the flood came and swept them all away, so too will be the coming of the Son of Man. Then two will be in the field; one will be taken and one will be left. Two women will be grinding meal together; one will be taken and one will be left. Keep awake therefore, for you do not know on what day your Lord is coming. But understand this: if the owner of the house had known in what part of the night the thief was coming, he would have stayed awake and would not have let his house be broken into. Therefore you also must be ready, for the Son of Man is coming at an unexpected hour."

MATTHEW 24:36–44

Jesus warned against getting anxiously upset by announcements of the end. Now he warns against complacently missing the signs of his arrival. In prayer we must be alert, but not gullible.

Do you have a lively sense of expectancy?

I never, O God, want to live in complacent sloth, soggy in religious routine, smug in pious satisfaction. I want to be expectant and ready for the new thing that you are doing today, and again tomorrow. Amen.

July 10

The Faithful and Wise Slave

"Who then is the faithful and wise slave, whom his master has put in charge of his household, to give the other slaves their allowance of food at the proper time? Blessed is that slave whom his master will find at work when he arrives. Truly I tell you, he will put that one in charge of all his possessions. But if that wicked slave says to himself, 'My master is delayed,' and he begins to beat his fellow slaves, and eats and drinks with drunkards, the master of that slave will come on a day when he does not expect him and at an hour that he does not know. He will cut him in pieces and put him with the hypocrites, where there will be weeping and gnashing of teeth."

MATTHEW 24:45–51

The ignorance of all of us (including the angels!) regarding the schedule of the coming again of Christ sets us free to go about our work of love without forever nervously checking the clock or calendar.

Do the predictors ever distract you from your work?

My curiosity, Lord, sometimes consumes me: I want to know when. And you draw me back into the fullness of this now, in which I can live by faith, content to receive what you give at the right time, and be steady at my work. Amen.

July 11

Ten Bridesmaids

"Ten bridesmaids took their lamps and went to meet the bridegroom. Five of them were foolish, and five were wise. When the foolish took their lamps, they took no oil with them; but the wise took flasks of oil. As the bridegroom was delayed, all of them became drowsy and slept. But at midnight there was a shout, 'Look! Here is the bridegroom! Come out to meet him.' The bridesmaids got up and trimmed their lamps. The foolish said to the wise, 'Give us some of your oil, for our lamps are going out.' But the wise replied, 'No! there will not be enough for you and for us; you had better go to the dealers and buy some for yourselves.' While they went to buy it, the bridegroom came, and those who were ready went with him into the wedding banquet; and the door was shut. Later the other bridesmaids came, saying, 'Lord, lord, open to us.' But he replied, 'Truly I tell you, I do not know you.' Keep awake therefore, for you know neither the day nor the hour."

MATTHEW 25:1–13

The parable asks, "What's smart?" rather than "What's right?" Our minds as well as our morals are to be put to proper use in expectation of Christ's coming. Foolishness is as much to be avoided in kingdom matters as wickedness.

How do you watch?

Dear God, you have given me careful teaching that you are coming, but not when, Keep me ever alert so that I am ready for whatever you have for me to do, whenever you choose to command me. Amen.

July 12

One Talent

"For it is as if a man, going on a journey, summoned his slaves and entrusted his property to them; to one he gave five talents, to another two, to another one, to each according to his ability. Then he went away. The one who had received the five talents went off at once and traded with them, and made five more talents. In the same way, the one who had the two talents made two more talents. But the one who had received the one talent went off and dug a hole in the ground and hid his master's money. After a long time the master of those slaves came and settled accounts with them. Then the one who had received the five talents came forward, bringing five more talents, saying, 'Master, you handed over to me five talents; see, I have made five more talents.' His master said to him, 'Well done, good and trustworthy slave; you have been trustworthy in a few things, I will put you in charge of many things; enter into the joy of your master.' And the one with the two talents also came forward, saying, 'Master, you handed over to me two talents; see, I have made two more talents.' His master said to him, 'Well done, good and trustworthy slave; you have been trustworthy in a few things, I will put you in charge of many things; enter into the joy of your master.' Then the one who had received the one talent also came forward, saying, 'Master, I knew that you were a harsh man, reaping where you did not sow, and gathering where you did not scatter seed; so I was afraid, and I went and hid your talent in the ground. Here you have what is yours.' But his master replied, 'You wicked and lazy slave! You knew, did you, that I reap where I did not sow, and gather where I did not scatter? Then you ought to have invested my money with the bankers, and on my return I would have received what was my own with interest. So take the talent from him, and give it to the one with the ten talents. For to all those who have, more will be given, and they will have an abundance; but from those who have nothing, even what they have will be taken away. As for this worthless slave, throw him into the outer darkness, where there will be weeping and gnashing of teeth.'"

Matthew 25:14–30

All of us have "one-talent" moods—times when it appears that everyone else has more than we do. We covet the more that others have, instead of devoting ourselves to use what we do have. Jesus has no patience with us at such times; his parable is a prod to live our lives, just as they are, to the glory of God.

Do you ever use your inadequacy as an excuse to do nothing?

Help me to accept my one-talent status, Lord, and be thankful for what you have given me. And help me to boldly participate in the exchanges of love that will make a profit for your kingdom. Amen.

Inherit the Kingdom

"When the Son of Man comes in his glory, and all the angels with him, then he will sit on the throne of his glory. All the nations will be gathered before him, and he will separate people one from another as a shepherd separates the sheep from the goats, and he will put the sheep at his right hand and the goats at the left. Then the king will say to those at his right hand, 'Come, you that are blessed by my Father, inherit the kingdom prepared for you from the foundation of the world; for I was hungry and you gave me food, I was thirsty and you gave me something to drink, I was a stranger and you welcomed me, I was naked and you gave me clothing, I was sick and you took care of me, I was in prison and you visited me.' Then the righteous will answer him, 'Lord, when was it that we saw you hungry and gave you food, or thirsty and gave you something to drink? And when was it that we saw you a stranger and welcomed you, or naked and gave you clothing? And when was it that we saw you sick or in prison and visited you?' And the king will answer them, 'Truly I tell you, just as you did it to one of the least of these who are members of my family, you did it to me.' Then he will say to those at his left hand, 'You that are accursed, depart from me into the eternal fire prepared for the devil and his angels; for I was hungry and you gave me no food, I was thirsty and you gave me nothing to drink. I was a stranger and you did not welcome me, naked and you did not give me clothing, sick and in prison and you did not visit me.' Then they also will answer, 'Lord, when was it that we saw you hungry or thirsty or a stranger or naked or sick or in prison, and did not take care of you?'

Then he will answer them, 'Truly I tell you, just as you did not do it to one of the least of these, you did not do it to me.' And these will go away into eternal punishment, but the righteous into eternal life."

MATTHEW 25:31–46

The great acts of judgment are not arbitrarily imposed from the outside, they develop out of the ordinary actions of everyday life. The final kingdom has all its seeds in the acts of love and compassion of each day.

Do you think you will be surprised at the last judgment?

Thank you for this parable, Jesus: now I know that everything counts. I will never again suppose that what I do is insignificant. I will look for your presence in every person I meet and serve you through them. Amen.

July 14

By Stealth

When Jesus had finished saying all these things, he said to his disciples. "You know that after two days the Passover is coming, and the Son of Man will be handed over to be crucified." Then the chief priests and the elders of the people gathered in the palace of the high priest, who was called Caiaphas, and they conspired to arrest Jesus by stealth and kill him. But they said, "Not during the festival, or there may be a riot among the people."

MATTHEW 26:1–5

While Jesus prophesied his death, his enemies plotted it. The rapt listening of the disciples is in contrast to the stealthy conspiracy of the high priests. The worlds in divided between those who hand on Jesus 'every word, and those who plot to eliminate him from their lives.

Why were the priests against Jesus?

Lord Jesus Christ, how grateful I am that you have entered the arena of suffering and hurt and evil. If all I had were words spoken from a quiet hillside, I would not have what I needed most—your victory over the worst, your presence in time of need. Amen.

July 15

Very Costly Ointment

Now while Jesus was at Bethany in the house of Simon the leper, a woman came to him with an alabaster jar of very costly ointment, and she poured it on his head as he sat at the table. But when the disciples saw it, they were angry and said, "Why this waste? For this ointment could have been sold for a large sum, and the money given to the poor." But Jesus, aware of this, said to them, "Why do you trouble the woman? She has performed a good service for me. For you always have the poor with you, but you will not always have me. By pouring this ointment on my body she has prepared me for burial. Truly I tell you, wherever this good news is proclaimed in the whole world, what she has done will be told in remembrance of her."

MATTHEW 26:6–13

Devout living is not tightfisted stinginess, but something flaming, with alabaster extravagance. We do not grow in faith by hoarding and saving, but by generous acts of sacrifice poured out in love.

Are you generous?

Save me, Lord Jesus, from the niggardly spirit that calculates and resents. Release me for a life that pours itself out without counting the cost, even as you poured yourself out for me. Amen.

July 16

Opportunity to Betray Him

Then one of the twelve, who was called Judas Iscariot, went to the chief priests and said, "What will you give me if I betray him to you?" They paid him thirty pieces of silver. And from that moment he began to look for an opportunity to betray him. . . . When it was evening, Jesus took his place with the twelve; and while they were eating, he said, "Truly I tell you, one of you will betray me." And they became greatly distressed and began to say to him one after another, "Surely not I, Lord?" He answered, "The one who has dipped his hand into the bowl with me will betray me. The Son of Man goes as it is written of him, but woe to that one by whom the Son of Man is betrayed! It would have been better for that one not to have been born." Judas, who betrayed him, said, "Surely not I, Rabbi?" He replied, "You have said so."

MATTHEW 26:14–25

It is difficult to comprehend that this act of betrayal could be committed by a man associated personally with Jesus, surrounded by peers in a common meal and intimate conversation. But any of us are capable of it: "It is I?" is an honest question to ask ourselves.

Why did Judas do it?

Forgive me, Father, for the times that I have suddenly left the way of faith and gone off to execute a plan that I thought would bring me some short-term benefit. Amen.

Took . . . Bread, . . . Took a Cup

While they were eating, Jesus took a loaf of bread, and after blessing it he broke it, gave it to the disciples, and said, "Take, eat; this is my body." Then he took a cup, and after giving thanks he gave it to them, saying, "Drink from it, all of you; for this is my blood of the covenant, which is poured out for many for the forgiveness of sins. I tell you, I will never again drink of this fruit of the vine until that day when I drink it new with you in my Father's kingdom."

MATTHEW 26:26–29

The common elements of the meal, through Jesus's words and prayer, became the signs of our eternal salvation. The deepest spiritual truths are represented in the everyday material of bread and wine.

What does the Lord's Supper mean to you?

I receive what you give to me, Lord Jesus Christ—your life and your salvation. As I receive it, I live in hope, anticipating the full life of the kingdom, even as I am participating in it now by your grace. Amen.

July 18

The Flock Will Be Scattered

When they had sung the hymn, they went out to the Mount of Olives. Then Jesus said to them, "You will all become deserters because of me this night; for it is written, 'I will strike the shepherd, and the sheep of the flock will be scattered.' But after I am raised up, I will go ahead of you to Galilee." Peter said to him, "Though all become deserters because of you, I will never desert you." Jesus said to him, "Truly I tell you, this very night, before the cock crows, you will deny me three times." Peter said to him, "Even though I must die with you, I will not deny you." And so said all the disciples.

MATTHEW 26:30–35

Stumbling was a way of life for Peter, as it is for us. Optimism in our capacity for faithfulness is not the basis of our salvation. Our trust is in the resurrection.

When was the last time you stumbled?

I am grateful, God, that your plans do not depend upon my loyalty, that your salvation is not contingent on my steadfastness. Your resurrection takes place anyway. All praise to you, O God. Amen.

July 19

Your Will Be Done

Then Jesus went with them to a place called Gethsemane; and he said to his disciples, "Sit here while I go over there and pray." . . . And going a little farther, he threw himself on the ground and prayed, "My Father, if it is possible, let this cup pass from me; yet not what I want but what you want." Then he came to the disciples and found them sleeping; and he said to Peter, "So, could you not stay awake with me one hour? Stay awake and pray that you may not come into the time of trial; the spirit indeed is willing, but the flesh is weak." Again he went away for the second time and prayed, "My Father, if this cannot pass unless I drink it, your will be done." Again he came and found them sleeping, for their eyes were heavy. So leaving them again, he went away and prayed for the third time, saying the same words. Then he came to the disciples and said to them, "Are you still sleeping and taking your rest? See, the hour is at hand, and the Son of Man is betrayed into the hands of sinners. Get up, let us be going. See, my betrayer is at hand."

MATTHEW 26:36–46

Sleeping, we slip into a private world, unconscious of God's action. Praying, the opposite of sleeping, explores every detail in the drama of existence, draws us into participation in Christ's passion.

What are some contracts between sleeping and praying?

Live in me, holy Christ; create a new Adam, a new Eve, to live to your glory in this garden. Teach me the freedom that lives your will instead of asserting my own. For Jesus's sake. Amen.

July 20

Deserted Him and Fled

While he was still speaking, Judas, one of the twelve, arrived; with him was a large crowd with swords and clubs, from the chief priests and the elders of the people. Now the betrayer had given them a sign, saying, "The one I will kiss is the man; arrest him." At once he came up to Jesus and said, "Greetings, Rabbi!" and kissed him. Jesus said to him, "Friend, do what you are here to do." Then they came and laid hands on Jesus and arrested him. . . . At that hour Jesus said to the crowds, "Have you come out with swords and clubs to arrest me as though I were a bandit? Day after day I sat in the temple teaching, and you did not arrest me. But all this has taken place, so that the scriptures of the prophets may be fulfilled." Then all the disciples deserted him and fled.

MATTHEW 26:47–56

Rome and religion conspired against Jesus and seized him, but he feared "no evil." He was so sure of God's "rod and staff" that he was confidently dismissive of all "swords and staves."

Where are you in this crowd?

You lived, Jesus, not by sword but by scripture. Yet I continue to use violence, even when I am attempting to do right things. Teach me to do it your way—your goals, yes, but also your methods. Amen.

July 21

Caiaphas ... Peter

Those who had arrested Jesus took him to Caiaphas the high priest, in whose house the scribes and the elders had gathered. But Peter was following him at a distance, as far as the courtyard of the high priest; ... Now the chief priests and the whole council were looking for false testimony against Jesus so that they might put him to death, but they found none, though many false witnesses came forward. ... But Jesus was silent. Then the high priest said to him, "I put you under oath before the living God, tell us if you are the Messiah, the Son of God." Jesus said to him, "You have said so. But I tell you, From now on you will see the Son of Man seated at the right hand of Power and coming on the clouds of heaven." Then the high priest tore his clothes and said, "He has blasphemed! Why do we still need witnesses? You have now heard his blasphemy. What is your verdict?" They answered, "He deserves death."

MATTHEW 26:57–66

Caiaphas and Peter are mentioned in successive sentences. The high priest and the chief apostle both center their attention on Jesus. Earlier, Peter had said "You are the Christ." Here, Caiaphas says it. The content of the gospel stays the same—but how different it sounds on the lips of Caiaphas and of Peter.

Why was Jesus silent?

A striking scene, Lord! The torture and mocking intended to reduce you to insignificance only reveal your strength. Out of this suffering your love appears with immense dignity and beauty. Thank You. Amen.

July 22

In the Beginning

In the beginning was the Word, and the Word was with God, and the Word was God.

JOHN 1:1

John and Genesis both fix our roots in God-reality: our origins are in the God who speaks (and is therefore intelligible to us) and whose speech (Word) makes the very stuff of our existence.

Compare John 1 with Genesis 1.

God of creation, let all my beginnings be in you: every thought, every act, every desire, every purpose, every plan. I would be rooted and grounded in you, and you only. Amen.

July 23

Made Through Him

He was in the beginning with God. All things came into being through him, and without him not one thing came into being. What has come into being . . .

JOHN 1:2–3

It is impossible to separate what we know of God from who God is, what God has said from his very being. Everything that is made is a clue leading to God, and God, of course, is the truth of everything.

How did creation take place?

Thank you, Lord, for this gloriously intricate, put-together, held-together universe. Everywhere I look I find evidence of what you have done. Everything I see gives me another reason to marvel and praise. Amen.

July 24

The Life Was the Light

... in him was life, and the life was the light of all people.

JOHN 1:4

Our ability to see anything and understand it is because of God. Even our questions about God are evidence of God. Our enlightened minds, which we may use to deny God, are a gift of the God who gives us life.

What are some characteristics of light?

Father of lights, in whom is no variableness, neither shadow of turning, I thank you for every good gift and every perfect gift come down from above in Jesus Christ (James 1:17). Amen.

Light/Darkness

The light shines in the darkness, and the darkness did not overcome it.

JOHN 1:5

In a contest between light and dark, light always wins. Darkness never smothers light; light always dissipates darkness. Darkness has no initiative and no energy. It is helpless against the pulsating radiance of the light.

What are some characteristics of darkness?

"This is the day of light: let there be light today; O Dayspring, rise upon our night and chase its gloom away." * Amen.

* John Ellerton, "This Is the Day of Light," *The Hymnbook*, 70.

July 26

Witness to the Light

There was a man sent from God, whose name was John. He came as a witness to testify to the light, so that all might believe through him. He himself was not the light, but he came to testify to the light.

JOHN 1:6–8

The contrast is abrupt: our minds are drawn from the wide, cosmic sweep of creation to the rough Judean wilderness, where a man is calling particular attention to God's work and word in Jesus Christ.

What do you know about John?

By your Word, God, the heavens were created; and by that same word I am addressed. What is going on in the heavens and in my home are equally your interest. Make the connection in my faith between your grand purposes and your specific involvement in my life. Amen.

The World Did Not Know Him

The true light, which enlightens everyone, was coming into the world. He was in the world, and the world came into being through him; yet the world did not know him. He came to what was his own, and his own people did not accept him.

John 1:9–11

That which is obvious in revelation and faith is not obvious to mere cleverness or doubt. "Think of it! The Word was made flesh and not one of the journalists of those days even knew it was happening!"*

Why was Jesus not recognized and not received?

Dear Lord, help me not to overlook the obvious—through carelessness miss the great signs of your saving love, through sloth have my eyes closed to the flashing lights of eternity, in Jesus Christ. Amen.

---

* G. Bernanos, *Diary of a Country Priest* (Garden City, NY: Image Books, 1954), 164.

Born . . . of God

But to all who received him, who believed in his name, he gave power to become children of God who were born, not of blood or of the will of the flesh or of the will of man, but of God.

JOHN 1:12–13

New birth is a theme that recurs throughout John's gospel. All that we know of birth, naturally, is a kind of parable of what God wills for us supernaturally.

Compare this with John 3:1–15.

Create, shape, and bring to maturity, Mighty God, the new life that you will for me in Jesus Christ. I want to be known as your child, be recognized as your child, and grow up into eternity as your child. Amen.

July 29

The Word Became Flesh

And the Word became flesh and lived among us, and we have seen his glory, the glory as of a father's only son, full of grace and truth.

JOHN 1:14

The "Word" by which God made all things (verses 1–3) became an actual flesh-and-blood person, Jesus of Nazareth. A most astounding event, scarcely imaginable, but impressively documented in our gospels by those who saw it take place ("we have beheld his glory").

Compare this with Galatians 4:4–5.

Father, open my eyes to see all that you reveal in Jesus Christ. I don't want to miss a single instance of grace, nor overlook one item of truth. I want to see it all, your glory in Jesus. Amen.

John Testified

John testified to him and cried out, "This was he of whom I said, 'He who comes after me ranks ahead of me because he was before me.'"

JOHN 1:15

John knew what to look for and what to expect—he was the first century's leading expert on the subject of Messiah. His years of preparatory preaching climaxed in his identification of Jesus as the Messiah sent and anointed by God.

How did John know that Jesus was the Messiah?

I thank you, dear God, for those teachers and preachers you have sent into my life to train me in what to look for and alert me to your living presence in Jesus Christ. Amen.

From His Fullness

From his fullness we have all received, grace upon grace. The law indeed was given through Moses; grace and truth came through Jesus Christ.

JOHN 1:16–17

God does not carefully calculate his stores of "grace and truth" and then cautiously dole them out in bits and pieces. He is lavish and extravagant as he reveals and shares himself in Jesus Christ.

What is "grace"?

God, what a change from what I was used to, living hand to mouth on morsels of law! Every day now is a banquet, grand and abundant! Thank you for this new life style of "grace upon grace." Amen.

August 1

The Only Son

No one has ever seen God. It is God the only Son, who is close to the Father's heart, who has made him known.

JOHN 1:18

In the words of Jesus, we know precisely what God says. In the actions of Jesus, we know accurately what God does. Jesus has taken all the guesswork out of thinking about and responding to God.

What does God look like?

God Almighty, whose ways are "past finding out," thank you for your plain speech in a language I can understand, and your forthright actions in forms to which I can respond, in Jesus. Amen.

I Am the Voice ...

This is the testimony given by John when the Jews sent priests and Levites from Jerusalem to ask him, "Who are you?" He confessed and did not deny it, but confessed, "I am not the Messiah." And they asked him, "What then? Are you Elijah?" He said, "I am not." "Are you the prophet?" He answered, "No." Then they said to him, "Who are you? Let us have an answer for those who sent us. What do you say about yourself?" He said, "I am the voice of one crying out in the wilderness, 'Make straight the way of the Lord,'" as the prophet Isaiah said.

JOHN 1:19–23

John attracted much attention and was prominent in the public eye. He could have used the attention and popularity to build himself a following. It didn't even occur to him: he had only one aim—to announce Jesus as the Christ.

What Isaiah passage does John cite?

When people pay attention to me, Lord, I am very apt to be flattered, pleased, and self-satisfied. Give me, instead, the grace to quickly refer all such interest to your love and grace and will in Jesus Christ. Amen.

August 3

Why Are You Baptizing?

Now they had been sent from the Pharisees. They asked him, "Why then are you baptizing if you are neither the Messiah, nor Elijah, nor the prophet?" John answered them, "I baptize with water. Among you stands one whom you do not know, the one who is coming after me; I am not worthy to untie the thong of his sandal." This took place in Bethany across the Jordan where John was baptizing.

JOHN 1:24–28

John's baptizing ministry fixed attention on our deepest need (sin) and God's greatest promise (forgiveness). But even while he did it, he made it clear that baptism was only sign-language—soon they would see and hear the actual words and authentic actions to which his ministry was mere prelude.

Why the reference to Elijah in the questions?

Don't let me ever, Lord Jesus Christ, get so interested in what others do in your name that I miss seeing your very presence; never so caught up in questions and answers that I fail to hear you speak to me personally. Amen.

August 4

Here Is the Lamb of God

The next day he saw Jesus coming toward him and declared, "Here is the Lamb of God who takes away the sin of the world! This is he of whom I said, 'After me comes a man who ranks ahead of me because he was before me.' I myself did not know him; but I came baptizing with water for this reason, that he might be revealed to Israel."

JOHN 1:29–31

The lamb was the animal most connected in Israel's mind with forgiveness. Its use in sacrificial worship demonstrated that God had a way of dealing with sin and guilt. When John identified Jesus as God's lamb, it meant that the great drama of forgiveness was about to take place before their eyes in him.

Compare this with Isaiah 53:7.

"When to the cross I turn my eyes, and rest on Calvary, O Lamb of God, my Sacrifice, I must remember Thee; remember Thee, and all Thy pains, and all Thy love to me: yea, while a breath, a pulse remains will I remember Thee." * Amen.

* James Montgomery, *The Hymnbook*, 373.

August 5

Like a Dove

And John testified, "I saw the Spirit descending from heaven like a dove, and it remained on him. I myself did not know him, but the one who sent me to baptize with water said to me, 'He on whom you see the Spirit descend and remain is the one who baptizes with the Holy Spirit.' And I myself have seen and have testified that this is the Son of God."

JOHN 1:32–34

The descent of the dove was a sign that the Spirit of God dwelt in Jesus—the very life of God the Father was also the very life of God the Son. John's witness of the sign authenticated Jesus's identity as Messiah.

What are the characteristics of a dove?

"Spirit of God, descend upon my heart; wean it from earth; through all its pulses move; stoop to my weakness, mighty as Thou art, and make me love Thee as I ought to love." * Amen.

---

* G. Croly, "Spirit of God, Descend Upon My Heart," *The Hymnbook*, 207.

Two Disciples

The next day John again was standing with two of his disciples, and as he watched Jesus walk by, he exclaimed, 'Look, here is the Lamb of God!' The two disciples heard him say this, and they followed Jesus. When Jesus turned and saw them following, he said to them, "What are you looking for?" They said to him, "Rabbi" (which translated means Teacher), "where are you staying?" He said to them, "Come and see." They came and saw where he was staying, and they remained with him that day. It was about four o'clock in the afternoon.

JOHN 1:35–39

The test of John's integrity came when the time arrived to turn his disciples over to Jesus. He passed the test: he knew he had finished his preparatory work, and so without reluctance turned those he had trained in repentance to follow Jesus in faith.

What is a disciple?

Help me, Lord Jesus, to be a good witness: quick to recognize your appearance, skilled at directing attention to you, and unhesitating in releasing people in my care to your care. Amen.

He First Found His Brother

One of the two who heard John speak and followed him was Andrew, Simon Peter's brother. He first found his brother Simon and said to him, "We have found the Messiah" (which is translated Anointed). He brought Simon to Jesus, who looked at him and said, "You are Simon son of John. You are to be called Cephas" (which is translated Peter).

JOHN 1:40–42

The first impulse of those who are attracted to Jesus is generosity—not to get all we can, exclusively, for ourselves, but to share all we can with others. Andrew's generosity was evangelism.

Whom have you brought to Jesus?

I want to be a good witness to you, Lord God, so that none among family or friends or neighbors may lack an invitation into your presence from rudeness or forgetfulness or selfishness on my part. Amen.

August 8

Nathanael

The next day Jesus decided to go to Galilee. He found Philip and said to him, "Follow me." Now Philip was from Bethsaida, the city of Andrew and Peter. Philip found Nathanael and said to him, "We have found him about whom Moses in the law and also the prophets wrote, Jesus son of Joseph from Nazareth." Nathanael said to him, "Can anything good come out of Nazareth?" Philip said to him, "Come and see." When Jesus saw Nathanael coming toward him, he said of him, "Here is truly an Israelite in whom there is no deceit!" Nathanael asked him, "Where did you get to know me?" Jesus answered, "I saw you under the fig tree before Philip called you." Nathanael replied, "Rabbi, you are the Son of God! You are the King of Israel!" Jesus answered, "Do you believe because I told you that I saw you under the fig tree? You will see greater things than these." And he said to him, "Very truly, I tell you, you will see heaven opened and the angels of God ascending and descending upon the Son of Man."

JOHN 1:43–51

Nathanael was an open book to Jesus—as are we all. His surprise at Jesus's comprehensive knowledge of his background and character led him to an immediate confession of faith.

What kind of person was Nathanael?

God, your spirit searches the depths in me: discovers sin, whets an appetite for righteousness, prompts obedience, kindles faith. Search me deeply; know me thoroughly, in Jesus. Amen.

August 9

A Wedding in Cana

There was a wedding in Cana of Galilee, and the mother of Jesus was there. . . . When the wine gave out, the mother of Jesus said to him, "They have no wine." And Jesus said to her, "Woman, what concern is that to you and to me? My hour has not yet come." His mother said to the servants, "Do whatever he tells you." Now standing there were six stone water jars, . . . each holding twenty or thirty gallons. Jesus said to them, "Fill the jars with water." And they filled them up to the brim. He said to them, "Now draw some out, and take it to the chief steward." So they took it. When the steward tasted the water that had become wine, and did not know where it came from, . . . the steward called the bridegroom and said to him, "Everyone serves the good wine first, and then the inferior wine after the guests have become drunk. But you have kept the good wine until now."

JOHN 2:1–10

As the first sign of Jesus's ministry, the miracle at Cana establishes joy at the center of all that Jesus does. Exuberance surrounds all our Lord's words and work. Salvation is life plus.

What was the result of the sign at Cana?

You do this a lot, Lord: just when I think there is nothing that can be done, with life reduced to mere survival and all resources (I think) exhausted, you step in and miraculously restore the joy, better than anything I thought possible. Thank you. Amen.

Capernaum ... for a Few Days

After this he went down to Capernaum with his mother, his brothers, and his disciples; and they remained there a few days.

JOHN 2:12

Jesus's work was not always in public, out where people could see it. There were also quiet interludes of retirement and rest. The quiet asides are as characteristic of his ministry as the glorious signs.

Where is Capernaum?

In this moment of quiet prayer, Father, so center my heart in your will and grace that all my actions and words today may flow from you as a cool stream from its subterranean source. Amen.

August 11

Zeal for Your House

The Passover of the Jews was near, and Jesus went up to Jerusalem. In the temple he found people selling cattle, sheep, and doves, and the money changers seated at their tables. Making a whip of cords, he drove all of them out of the temple, both the sheep and the cattle. He also poured out the coins of the money changers and overturned their tables. He told those who were selling the doves, "Take these things out of here! Stop making my Father's house a marketplace!" His disciples remembered that it was written, "Zeal for your house will consume me."

JOHN 2:13–17

Religion is easily and commonly commercialized. Each church needs repeated and vigorous temple-cleansings to restore it to its proper function as a center for prayer.

Where does the "zeal for Thy house" quotation come from?

Lord God of hosts, invade our cluttered churches, clogged with religious baggage, and do a good housecleaning among us so that there is room for the one thing needful, for prayer. Amen.

August 12

The Temple of His Body

The Jews then said to him, "What sign can you show us for doing this?" Jesus answered them, "Destroy this temple, and in three days I will raise it up." The Jews then said, "This temple has been under construction for forty-six years, and will you raise it up in three days?" But he was speaking of the temple of his body. After he was raised from the dead, his disciples remembered that he had said this; and they believed the scripture and the word that Jesus had spoken.

JOHN 2:18–22

The body of Jesus took over the functions of the Jerusalem temple, centering attention on God's presence among his people, providing a focus for sacrifice and adoration, and best of all, showing forth the resurrection.

Compare this with 1 Corinthians 6:19.

Just as your body, Lord Jesus, was a temple, make mine also a temple—a place where your spirit dwells, a place to glorify God, a place for crucifixion and resurrection. Amen.

August 13

He Knew All People

When he was in Jerusalem during the Passover festival, many believed in his name because they saw the signs that he was doing. But Jesus on his part would not entrust himself to them, because he knew all people and needed no one to testify about anyone; for he himself knew what was in everyone.

JOHN 2:23–25

Jesus did not plot his course on the basis of popular opinion polls. The response of the crowds played no part in guiding his ministry. God provided the compass points for his journey.

At what seasons of the year does Passover come?

All the things that, in my naivete, seem so important to me—acclaim, enthusiasm, success, acceptance—are on the periphery of your ministry, Lord Jesus. You march to a different drummer. Give me ears to hear that drum beat, too. Amen.

August 14

Born Anew

Now there was a Pharisee named Nicodemus, a leader of the Jews. He came to Jesus by night and said to him, "Rabbi, we know that you are a teacher who has come from God; for no one can do these signs that you do apart from the presence of God." Jesus answered him, "Very truly, I tell you, no one can see the kingdom of God without being born from above." Nicodemus said to him, "How can anyone be born after having grown old? Can one enter a second time into the mother's womb and be born?" Jesus answered, "Very truly, I tell you, no one can enter the kingdom of God without being born of water and Spirit. What is born of the flesh is flesh, and what is born of the Spirit is spirit. Do not be astonished that I said to you, 'You must be born from above.'"

JOHN 3:1–7

B irth is a sudden and violent transition from the womb to the world, from darkness to light—and explosion into humanity (the world of the "flesh"). New birth is the same transition into the reality of God.

Have you been born anew?

Spirit of God, breathe through my existence and bring new life to every part of it: open my eyes to the light of salvation, make me conversant with the truth of faith; guide me in the growth of holiness, in Jesus Christ. Amen.

August 15

The Wind Blows Where It Chooses

"The wind blows where it chooses, and you hear the sound of it, but you do not know where it comes from or where it goes. So it is with everyone who is born of the Spirit."

JOHN 3:8

"Wind" and "spirit" are the same word in Greek. Neither is visible, but what they produce is visible. Will we believe that which we cannot see? We do it all the time with the wind; why don't we do it with the Spirit?

What do you know about the Spirit?

I look to you, O God, whom I do not see, to renew all that I do see. Even while I am immersed in the world of the senses, I put my trust in the world of the Spirit, where all strength, love and redemption originate. Amen.

August 16

How Can These Things Be?

Nicodemus said to him, "How can these things be?" Jesus answered him, "Are you a teacher of Israel, and yet you do not understand these things? Very truly, I tell you, we speak of what we know and testify to what we have seen; yet you do not receive our testimony. If I have told you about earthly things and you do not believe, how can you believe if I tell you about heavenly things? No one has ascended into heaven except the one who descended from heaven, the Son of Man. And just as Moses lifted up the serpent in the wilderness, so must the Son of Man be lifted up that whoever believes in him may have eternal life."

JOHN 3:9–15

There is much that we can understand about God's ways, but also much that we cannot. God's ways do not contradict our reason, but they do exceed our reason. The revelation that Christ ("he whom descended") brings to us puts all the bits and pieces of our knowledge into a complete truth.

How does the reference to Moses help?

My questions and all knowledge barely make a dent in what I need to know, O Christ: tell me all I need to know; show me what I need to do: complete my understanding with your revelation. Amen.

August 17

God So Loved the World

"For God so loved the world that he gave his only Son, so that everyone who believes in him may not perish but may have eternal life."

JOHN 3:16

The verse is deservedly famous: from it we learn God's attitude toward us (love), his action among us (he gave his Son), and his purpose for us (eternal life). Everything we need to know about God—and all of it is good.

When did you first learn this verse?

"Love divine, all loves excelling, joy of heaven, to earth come down, fix in us Thy humble dwelling, all Thy faithful mercies crown! Jesus, Thou art all compassion, pure, unbounded love Thou art; visit us with Thy salvation, enter every trembling heart" * Amen.

* Charles Wesley, "Love Divine, All Loves Excelling," *The Hymnbook*, 337.

This Is the Judgment

"Indeed, God did not send the Son into the world to condemn the world, but in order that the world might be saved through him. Those who believe in him are not condemned; but those who do not believe are condemned already, because they have not believed in the name of the only Son of God. And this is the judgment, that the light has come into the world, and people loved darkness rather than light because their deeds were evil. For all who do evil hate the light and do not come to the light, so that their deeds may not be exposed. But those who do what is true come to the light, so that it may be clearly seen that their deeds have been done in God."

JOHN 3:17–21

Judgment is not an arbitrary lashing out from a despotic deity; it is self-inflicted. It follows from the deliberate, conscious choice of darkness over light, of evil instead of good.

What is the judgment?

Thank you, gracious Father, for relieving me of fears, but not of responsibility, for banishing my anxiety without robbing me of the dignity of decision, in the name of Jesus Christ, my Savior. Amen.

August 19

Baptizing at Aenon

After this Jesus and his disciples went into the Judean countryside, and the spent some time there with them and baptized. John also was baptizing at Aenon near Salim because water was abundant there; and people kept coming and were being baptized—John, of course, had not yet been thrown into prison.

JOHN 3:22–24

The ministries of John and Jesus overlapped at Aenon, an obscure spring along the Jordan, in the magnificent practice of baptism—a sign of turning away from sin in repentance and evidence of turning toward God in faith. Baptism linked the two ministries so that nothing of value in John's ministry was lost in the full exercise of Jesus's ministry.

How is baptism an appropriate link?

Great God: such great acts of ministry! and in such ordinary, everyday places! Continue to do your great works in the kitchen and family room and bedrooms of my house, and among the neighbors on my street. In Jesus's name. Amen.

August 20

_____

. . . I Must Decrease

Now a discussion about purification arose between John's disciples and a Jew. They came to John and said to him, "Rabbi, the one who was with you across the Jordan, to whom you testified, here he is baptizing, and all are going to him." John answered, "No one can receive anything except what has been given from heaven. You yourselves are my witnesses that I said, 'I am not the Messiah, but I have been sent ahead of him.' He who has the bride is the bridegroom. The friend of the bridegroom, who stands and hears him, rejoices greatly at the bridegroom's voice. For this reason my joy has been fulfilled. He must increase, but I must decrease."

JOHN 3:25–30

John, used to being at the center of attention was ready, on signal, to step out of the spotlight into the shadows. All ministry is Christ's. There can be no competition or rivalry among people who are working God's will, even when they are working along different lines.

Do you think it was difficult for John to take second place?

Dear Jesus, teach me my place: as a servant, not a master, as the friend of the bridegroom, not the bridegroom; as a witness to the truth, not the truth itself. Amen.

August 21

He Who Comes from Heaven

The one who comes from above is above all; the one who is of the earth belongs to the earth and speaks about earthly things. The one who comes from heaven is above all. He testifies to what he has seen and heard, yet no one accepts his testimony. Whoever has accepted his testimony has certified this, that God is true. He whom God has sent speaks the words of God, for he gives the Spirit without measure. The Father loves the Son and has placed all things in his hands. Whoever believes in the Son has eternal life; whoever disobeys the Son will not see life, but must endure God's wrath.

JOHN 3:31–36

Jesus is not just a better version of Moses, or David, or Elijah—or John. He is different entirely: "from heaven." Jesus is not a word about God, but the very word of God. His presence brings us into the fullness of God. In him we have not just a fragment of truth but the whole picture of redemption.

What is the difference between John and Jesus?

I receive of your fullness, O God in Christ: increase my capacity to believe, to obey, and to enjoy. I will not be content with hand-me-down truth or secondhand faith. I want it fresh and whole. Amen.

August 22

Jacob's Well

Now when Jesus learned that the Pharisees had heard, "Jesus is making and baptizing more disciples than John"—although it was not Jesus himself but his disciples who baptized—he left Judea and started back to Galilee. But he had to go through Samaria. So he came to a Samaritan city called Sychar, near the plot of ground that Jacob had given to his son Joseph. Jacob's well was there, and Jesus, tired out by his journey, was sitting by the well. It was about noon.

JOHN 4:1–6

For over seven hundred years, racial hostility existed between Samaritans and Jews. But a thousand years before that, Jacob, a common ancestor, had dug a well from which they both drank. If we go back far enough in history, we find sources of a common heritage.

What time of day was the sixth hour?

Lord, plunge us in Jordan's baptismal stream, dig us a deep Samaritan well, waters to wash the guilt from our land: cleanse us and sing our peace. Amen.

August 23

If You Knew the Gift of God

A Samaritan woman came to draw water, and Jesus said to her, "Give me a drink." (His disciples had gone to the city to buy food.) The Samaritan woman said to him, "How is it that you, a Jew, ask a drink of me, a woman of Samaria?" (Jews do not share things in common with Samaritans.) Jesus answered her, "If you knew the gift of God, and who it is that is saying to you, 'Give me a drink,' you would have asked him, and he would have given you living water."

JOHN 4:7–10

Jesus begins the conversation by asking for something; he will end it by giving something: his asking is always preparatory to his giving. Our relationship with God changes radically when we realize the "gift" nature of his being: he does not harass us with petty requests but offers us a magnificent gift.

What is the "gift of God"?

Deepen my sense of need, dear Christ: enlarge my expectations of your gifts. Help me to see faith not so much as that which I give you, but as that which you give me—even eternal life. Amen.

August 24

Give Me This Water

The woman said to him, "Sir, you have no bucket, and the well is deep. Where do you get that living water? Are you greater than our ancestor Jacob, who gave us the well, and with his sons and his flocks drank from it?" Jesus said to her, "Everyone who drinks of this water will be thirsty again but those who drink of the water that I will give them will never be thirsty. The water that I will give will become in them a spring of water gushing up to eternal life." The woman said to him, "Sir, give me this water, so that I may never be thirsty or have to keep coming here to draw water."

JOHN 4:11–15

Misunderstanding does not always prevent communication; sometimes, as in this case, it is a creative stimulus to pursue complete understanding. Jesus uses the physical as a basis of awakening desire for the spiritual.

Compare with Matthew 5:6.

Give me this water, Lord Jesus: satisfy my spirit at the deep well of eternal life, springing up abundantly. Let me drink of it daily and always, and never thirst again. Amen.

August 25

Worship in Spirit and Truth

Jesus said to her, "Go, call your husband, and come back." The woman answered him, "I have no husband." Jesus said to her, "You are right in saying, 'I have no husband'; for you have had five husbands, and the one you have now is not your husband. . . ." The woman said to him, "Sir, I see that you are a prophet. Our ancestors worshiped on this mountain, but you say that the place where people must worship is in Jerusalem." Jesus said to her, "Woman, believe me, . . . the hour is coming, and is now here, when the true worshipers will worship the Father in spirit and truth, for the Father seeks such as these to worship him. God is spirit, and those who worship him must worship in spirit and truth." The woman said to him, "I know that Messiah is coming" (who is called Christ). "When he comes, he will proclaim all things to us." Jesus said to her, "I am he, the one who is speaking to you."

JOHN 4:16–26

The conversation intensifies as the discussion moves from getting water out of a well to worshiping God. The woman is led into an awareness of her interior needs and of God's ultimate fulfillments.

What does this tell you about worship?

God, I don't want to get hung up on questions of the places for worship or the times to worship or the forms of worship: I want to worship, inwardly, ardently, and truly, and so discover you as the center of my life, in Jesus Christ. Amen.

August 26

Ripe for Harvesting

Just then his disciples came. They were astonished that he was speaking with a woman, but no one said, "What do you want?" or, "Why are you speaking with her?" Then the woman left her water jar and went back to the city. She said to the people, "Come and see a man who told me everything I have ever done! He cannot be the Messiah, can he?" They left the city and were on their way to him. Meanwhile the disciples were urging him, "Rabbi, eat something." But he said to them, "I have food to eat that you do not know about." So the disciples said to one another, "Surely no one has brought him something to eat?" Jesus said to them, "My food is to do the will of him who sent me and to complete his work. Do you not say, 'Four months more, then comes the harvest'? But I tell you, look around you, and see how the fields are ripe for harvesting."

JOHN 4:27–35

The description of the Samaritans as a field ripe for harvest must have been a surprise! The usual Jewish view was that they were no more than a vacant lot, filled with rubble. Jesus removed the blinders of prejudice from our eyes so that we can see truly.

Compare this with 1 Corinthians 3:6–9.

Forgive me, Lord, for rejecting people whom I suppose are not interested in your love, and for avoiding others whom I think will revile your grace. Where I see a field of weeds you see a field ripe for harvest. Help me to see it your way. Amen.

August 27

Your Son Will Live

Then he came again to Cana in Galilee where he had changed the water into wine. Now there was a royal official whose son lay ill in Capernaum. When he heard that Jesus had come from Judea to Galilee, he went and begged him to come down and heal his son, for he was at the point of death. Then Jesus said to him, "Unless you see signs and wonders you will not believe." The official said to him, "Sir, come down before my little boy dies." Jesus said to him, "Go; your son will live." The man believed the word that Jesus spoke to him and started on his way. As he was going down, his slaves met him and told him that his child was alive. So he asked them the hour when he began to recover, and they said to him, "Yesterday at one in the afternoon the fever left him." The father realized that this was the hour when Jesus had said to him, "Your son will live." So he himself believed, along with his whole household.

JOHN 4:46–53

The official believed before he saw. He did not require "signs and wonders" as a condition for his trust. He had nothing to sustain him on his trip homeward but the word of Jesus. He believed simply because Jesus spoke.

How far is it from Cana to Capernaum?

Jesus, speak the word that will put my faith in motion; then send me back to the sphere of my obedience and raise my expectations for the fulfillment of your promises. Amen.

August 28

I Have No One

After this there was a festival of the Jews, and Jesus went up to Jerusalem. Now in Jerusalem by the Sheep Gate there is a pool, called in Hebrew Beth-zatha, which has five porticoes. In these lay many invalids—blind, lame, and paralyzed. One man was there who had been ill for thirty-eight years. When Jesus saw him lying there and knew that he had been there a long time, he said to him, "Do you want to be made well?" The sick man answered him, "Sir, I have no one to put me into the pool when the water is stirred up; and while I am making my way, someone else steps down ahead of me." Jesus said to him, "Stand up, take your mat and walk." At once the man was made well, and he took up his mat and began to walk. Now that day was a sabbath.

JOHN 5:1–9

The helpless sick man had been within sight of help throughout his illness. He knew he needed help; he knew help was available; but he couldn't help himself. Jesus helps those who can't help themselves.

What can't you do for yourself?

"I sought the Lord, and afterward I knew He moved my soul to seek Him, seeking me; it was not I that found, O Savior true; no, I was found of Thee." * Amen.

* Anonymous.

254

August 29

Equal to God

So the Jews said to the man who had been cured, "It is the sabbath; it is not lawful for you to carry your mat." But he answered them, "The man who made me well said to me, 'Take up your mat and walk.'" They asked him, "Who is the man who said to you, 'Take it up and walk'?" Now the man who had been healed did not know who it was, for Jesus had disappeared in the crowd that was there. Later Jesus found him in the temple and said to him, "See, you have been made well! Do not sin any more, so that nothing worse happens to you." The man went away and told the Jews that it was Jesus who had made him well. Therefore the Jews started persecuting Jesus, because he was doing such things on the sabbath. But Jesus answered them, "My Father is still working, and I also am working." For this reason the Jews were seeking all the more to kill him, because he was not only breaking the sabbath, but was also calling God his own Father.

JOHN 5:10–18

Far from misunderstanding Jesus, his persecutors understood precisely what was involved: that Jesus, by healing on the Sabbath and calling God his Father, was the very presence of God among them. But they preferred to keep God at a distance.

How close do you want God to you?

I do this too, Lord: I acknowledge you, but want you to work only within the framework I have constructed; I believe in you, but get uncomfortable when you get involved in my affairs. Forgive me. Amen.

August 30

The Son Gives Life

Jesus said to them, "Very truly, I tell you, the Son can do nothing on his own, but only what he sees the Father doing; for whatever the Father does, the Son does likewise. The Father loves the Son and shows him all that he himself is doing; and he will show him greater works than these, so that you will be astonished. Indeed, just as the Father raises the dead and gives them life, so also the Son gives life to whomever he wishes."

JOHN 5:19–21

God the Father and God the son, the God they could not see and the Christ they saw right before them, were, for all practical purposes, the same. The function of the one was to audibly reveal the mind and visibly execute the will of the other.

What were the "greater works"?

I offer you my adoration and my obedience, Lord Jesus. By your life I discover redemption; in your words I find direction; through your resurrection I enjoy eternal life. All praise to your great name! Amen.

August 31

That All May Honor the Son

The Father judges no one but has given all judgment to the Son, so that all may honor the Son just as they honor the Father. Anyone who does not honor the Son does not honor the Father who sent him. Very truly, I tell you, anyone who hears my word and believes him who sent me has eternal life, and does not come under judgment, but has passed from death to life.

JOHN 5:22–24

It does no good to say that we honor God if we dishonor him in our actions. God is not a far-off idea that we venerate in pious moments; he is an actual presence that we respond to in the historical now of Jesus Christ.

How do you honor God?

"Blessing and honor and glory and power, wisdom and riches and strength evermore give ye to Him who our battle hath won, whose are the Kingdom, the crown, and the throne." * Amen.

* H. Bonar, "Blessing and Honor and Glory and Power," *The Hymnbook,* 125.

September 1

The Dead Will Hear the Voice

"Very truly, I tell you, the hour is coming, and is now here, when the dead will hear the voice of the Son of God, and those who hear will live. For just as the Father has life in himself, so he has granted the Son also to have life in himself; and he has given him authority to execute judgment, because he is the Son of Man. Do not be astonished at this; for the hour is coming when all who are in their graves will hear his voice and will come out—those who have done good, to the resurrection of life, and those who have done evil, to the resurrection of condemnation."

JOHN 5:25–29

The words of Jesus are not pious embroidery for religious pillows. The ministry of Jesus is radical and it is ultimate: it crashes the boundaries of death and summons all to a resurrection.

What happens at resurrection?

I hear thunder in your speech, O God; I see lightning in your acts. Storm through this soul of mine, wake the sleeping parts of me; raise the dead parts of me; stand me on my feet, alert and praising in your presence. Amen.

September 2

If You Believed Moses …

"I can do nothing on my own. As I hear, I judge; and my judgment is just, because I seek to do not my own will but the will of him who sent me. If I testify about myself, my testimony is not true. There is another who testifies on my behalf, and I know that his testimony to me is true. You sent messengers to John, and he testified to the truth. Not that I accept such human testimony, but I say these things so that you may be saved. He was a burning and shining lamp, and you were willing to rejoice for a while in his light. But I have a testimony greater than John's. The works that the Father has given me to complete, the very works that I am doing, testify on my behalf that the Father has sent me. And the Father who sent me has himself testified on my behalf. You have never heard his voice or seen his form, and you do not have his word abiding in you, because you do not believe him whom he has sent. You search the scriptures because you think that in them you have eternal life; and it is they that testify on my behalf. Yet you refuse to come to me to have life. I do not accept glory from human beings. But I know that you do not have the love of God in you. I have come in my Father's name, and you do not accept me; if another comes in his own name, you will accept him. How can you believe when you accept glory from one another and do not seek the glory that comes from the one who alone is God? Do not think that I will accuse you before the Father; your accuser is Moses, on whom you have set your hope. If you believed Moses, you would believe me, for he wrote about me. But if you do not believe what he wrote, how will you believe what I say?"

John 5:30–47

Everything converges to authenticate Jesus as God's Christ: the ministry of John the Baptist (vv. 33–35); the "very works," which anyone can observe and evaluate (vv. 36–38); and the authoritative scriptures (vv. 39–47). The evidence is massive. Those who refuse to believe Jesus refuse on the grounds of sin, not logic.

What convinced you to believe in Jesus?

So far as I am able, Lord, I want to grasp the grand sweep of your reality and perceive each sharply etched detail of your presence. Use all the evidence—what others say about you, what you say about yourself, what the scriptures say about you—to both enlarge and sharpen my faith. Amen.

September 3

Then Jesus Took the Loaves

When he looked up and saw a large crowd coming toward him, Jesus said to Philip, "Where are we to buy bread for these people to eat?" . . . Philip answered him, "Six months' wages would not buy enough bread for each of them to get a little." One of his disciples, Andrew, Simon Peter's brother, said to him, "There is a boy here who has five barley loaves and two fish. But what are they among so many people?" Jesus said, "Make the people sit down." Now there was a great deal of grass in the place; so they sat down, about five thousand in all. Then Jesus took the loaves, and when he had given thanks, he distributed them to those who were seated; so also the fish, as much as they wanted. When they were satisfied, he told his disciples, "Gather up the fragments left over, so that nothing may be lost." So they gathered them up, and from the fragments of the five barley loaves, left by those who had eaten, they filled twelve baskets.

JOHN 6:5–13

Jesus's feeding of the five thousand is a sign of both his intention and his ability to provide for us whatever we need. His care is all-inclusive. His power is unrestricted. Body and spirit are equally sustained by his command.

What material difference does Jesus make in your life?

In the meals I eat today, O God, I will receive your gifts. My Food is evidence of what you make and what you give. Thank you for bread and fish, in Jesus's name. Amen.

September 4

The Food That Endures

His disciples went down to the sea, got into a boat, and started across the sea to Capernaum. It was now dark, and Jesus had not yet come to them. The sea became rough because a strong wind was blowing. When they had rowed about three or four miles, they saw Jesus walking on the sea and coming near the boat, and they were terrified. But he said to them, "It is I; do not be afraid." . . . When [the crowd] found him, they said to him, "Rabbi, when did you come here?" Jesus answered them, "Very truly, I tell you, you are looking for me, not because you saw signs, but because you ate your fill of the loaves. Do not work for the food that perishes, but for the food that endures for eternal life, which the Son of Man will give you. For it is on him that God the Father has set his seal." Then they said to him, "What must we do to perform the works of God?" Jesus answered them, "This is the work of God, that you believe in him whom he has sent."

JOHN 6:16–29

We can work for trivial ends or eternal ends. We can labor for that which passes away or for that which lasts forever. It is not a question of whether we work or not—we must work in either case—the question is, "Who will we work for?"

Who do you work for?

I put myself under your orders today, Lord Jesus. As I go to work, let me do everything in obedience to you and for the glory of your name, knowing that nothing is too slight or out of the way to be used to your glory. Amen.

September 5

Bread from Heaven

So they said to him, "What sign are you going to give us then, so that we may see it and believe you? What work are you performing? Our ancestors ate the manna in the wilderness; as it is written, 'He gave them bread from heaven to eat.'" Then Jesus said to them, "Very truly, I tell you, it was not Moses who gave you the bread from heaven, but it is my Father who gives you the true bread from heaven. For the bread of God is that which comes down from heaven and gives life to the world." They said to him, "Sir, give us this bread always."

JOHN 6:30–34

The people were right in connecting the manna in the wilderness with the feeding of the five thousand. But they were wrong in stopping there; by so doing they were missing the profound provisions by God to satisfy their soul's hunger.

God, I know that my entire life is surrounded by your providence and upheld by your mercy: I thank you for all that you give me, bread from the bakery and bread from heaven, satisfying my body and my spirit. Amen.

September 6

I Am the Bread of Life

Jesus said to them, "I am the bread of life. Whoever comes to me will never be hungry, and whoever believes in me will never be thirsty. But I said to you that you have seen me and yet do not believe. Everything that the Father gives me will come to me, and anyone who comes to me I will never drive away; for I have come down from heaven, not to do my own will, but the will of him who sent me. And this is the will of him who sent me, that I should lose nothing of all that he has given me, but raise it up on the last day. This is indeed the will of my Father, that all who see the Son and believe in him may have eternal life; and I will raise them up on the last day."

JOHN 6:35–40

Jesus is our staple product. Received into our lives, like bread, he is the basic stuff of life for us. In him the essential needs of the day are satisfied and the central purposes in eternity are fulfilled.

How is Jesus like bread?

"Break Thou the bread of life, dear Lord, to me, as Thou didst break the loaves beside the sea; beyond the sacred page I seek Thee, Lord; my spirit pants for Thee, O Living Word!" * Amen.

* Mary A. Lathbury, "Bread Thou the Bread of Life," *The Hymnbook,* 219.

Do Not Complain

Then the Jews began to complain about him because he said, "I am the bread that came down from heaven." They were saying, "Is not this Jesus, the son of Joseph, whose father and mother we know? How can he now say, 'I have come down from heaven'?" Jesus answered them, "Do not complain among yourselves. No one can come to me unless drawn by the Father who sent me; and I will raise that person up on the last day. It is written in the prophets, 'And they shall all be taught by God.' Everyone who has heard and learned from the Father comes to me. Not that anyone has seen the Father except the one who is from God; he has seen the Father."

JOHN 6:41–46

The conventional imagination reeled and rocked under the impact of Jesus's claim. The proclamation that God was actually present among them was staggering—and they staggered.

What scripture does Jesus quote?

I bring such small-minded and cramped ideas to my encounters with you, Lord. And you come to me filling the air with a vast love and an immense grace! Stretch my mind to take in all that you are; enlarge my spirit to respond to all that you give, in Jesus Christ. Amen.

September 8

Down from Heaven

"Very truly, I tell you, whoever believes has eternal life. I am the bread of life. Your ancestors ate the manna in the wilderness, and they died. This is the bread that comes down from heaven, so that one may eat of it and not die. I am the living bread that came down from heaven. Whoever eats of this bread will live forever; and the bread that I will give for the life of the world is my flesh."

John 6:47–51

Life comes from above—not from around and not from within. Eternal salvation is a gift from God, not an accumulation of human virtue. We get what we need eternally by opening ourselves to God and receiving what he gives in Christ, not by trying to make it on our own.

What happened in the wilderness?

Dear Lord God, I don't want to live on the memory of old miracles, but experience fresh ones in faith. Draw me into the fullness of this day's grace in which you have new things to do in and through me, in Jesus. Amen.

September 9

How ... ?

The Jews then disputed among themselves, saying, "How can this man give us his flesh to eat?" So Jesus said to them, "Very truly, I tell you, unless you eat the flesh of the Son of Man and drink his blood, you have no life in you. Those who eat my flesh and drink my blood have eternal life, and I will raise them up on the last day; for my flesh is true food and my blood is true drink. Those who eat my flesh and drink my blood abide in me, and I in them. Just as the living Father sent me, and I live because of the Father, so whoever eats me will live because of me. This is the bread that came down from heaven, not like that which your ancestors ate, and they died. But the one who eats this bread will live forever." He said these things while he was teaching in the synagogue at Capernaum.

JOHN 6:52–59

Jesus does not answer questions, he asks them. He is not a puzzle for us to figure out, but the very life of God in the form we can receive it. Coming to Jesus is not entering a classroom, but sitting down at a banquet.

Do your questions ever get in the way of your faith?

Father, your gifts are beyond my understanding; your life exceeds my ability to explain it. But explanations are not what I really want anyway. What I really want are deepened capacities to receive and enjoy, through Jesus Christ. Amen.

This Teaching Is Difficult

When many of his disciples heard it, they said, "This teaching is difficult; who can accept it?" But Jesus, being aware that his disciples were complaining about it, said to them, "Does this offend you? Then what if you were to see the Son of Man ascending to where he was before? It is the spirit that gives life; the flesh is useless. The words that I have spoken to you are spirit and life. But among you there are some who do not believe." For Jesus knew from the first who were the ones that did not believe, and who was the one that would betray him. And he said, "For this reason I have told you that no one can come to me unless it is granted by the Father."

JOHN 6:60–65

The difficulty is not in what we must do, but what we must not do—namely, attempt to be gods or goddesses on our own. It is a lovely ambition and hard to give up. But until we do we cannot accept Christ as Lord and Savior.

Why do some still not believe?

Lord, you dash my fondest dreams—dreams of being in control of my life, dreams of controlling others. Then you give something far better—the vision of your lordship and redemption. Banish unbelief from my heart and grant, in your mercy, faith. Amen.

Do You Also Wish to Go Away?

Because of this many of his disciples turned back and no longer went about with him. So Jesus asked the twelve, "Do you also wish to go away?" Simon Peter answered him, "Lord, to whom can we go? You have the words of eternal life. We have come to believe and know that you are the Holy One of God." Jesus answered them, "Did I not choose you, the twelve? Yet one of you is a devil." He was speaking of Judas son of Simon Iscariot, for he, though one of the twelve, was going to betray him.

JOHN 6:66–71

Jesus trusts us with the big eternity-shaping decisions. He will not force us into virtue; he will not compel faith; he will not coerce us into discipleship. Following Jesus is a true and deep act of freedom.

What is the difference between Peter and Judas?

Lord Jesus Christ, keep me from wandering, from turning back, from quitting. By your grace "I press on toward the goal for the prize of the upward call of God in Christ Jesus." Amen.

September 12

Not Even His Brothers Believed

After this Jesus went about in Galilee. He did not wish to go about in Judea because the Jews were looking for an opportunity to kill him. Now the Jewish festival of Booths was near. So his brothers said to him, "Leave here and go to Judea so that your disciples also may see the works you are doing; for no one who wants to be widely known acts in secret. If you do these things, show yourself to the world." (For not even his brothers believed in him.) Jesus said to them, "My time has not yet come, but your time is always here. The world cannot hate you, but it hates me because I testify against it that its works are evil. Go to the festival yourselves. I am not going to this festival, for my time has not yet fully come." After saying this, he remained in Galilee.

JOHN 7:1–9

Unbelief is impatient with God's ways. The counsel of Jesus 'brothers stemmed not from their trust in him, but from their doubts about him. But Jesus will not be hurried, and he will not be pushed.

What kind of feast was Tabernacles?

Do it your way, Jesus, and in your time. Give me the gift of patience to wait, the gift of courage to persevere, and the gift of faith to believe that you do all things right. Amen.

My Teaching Is Not Mine

But after his brothers had gone to the festival, then he also went, not publicly but as it were in secret. The Jews were looking for him at the festival and saying, "Where is he?" And there was considerable complaining about him among the crowds. While some were saying, "He is a good man," others were saying, "No, he is deceiving the crowd." Yet no one would speak openly about him for fear of the Jews. About the middle of the festival Jesus went up into the temple and began to teach. The Jews were astonished at it, saying, "How does this man have such learning, when he has never been taught?" Then Jesus answered them, "My teaching is not mine but his who sent me. Anyone who resolves to do the will of God will know whether the teaching is from God or whether I am speaking on my own. Those who speak on their own seek their own glory; but the one who seeks the glory of him who sent him is true, and there is nothing false in him. Did not Moses give you the law? Yet none of you keeps the law. Why are you looking for an opportunity to kill me?" The crowd answered, "You have a demon! Who is trying to kill you?" Jesus answered them, "I performed one work, and all of you are astonished. Moses gave you circumcision (it is, of course, not from Moses, but from the patriarchs), and you circumcise a man on the sabbath. If a man receives circumcision on the sabbath in order that the law of Moses may not be broken, are you angry with me because I healed a man's whole body on the sabbath? Do not judge by appearances, but judge with right judgment."

JOHN 7:10–24

The authority that everyone senses in Jesus's teaching is unaccountable in terms of human learning. He does not speak about God, giving secondhand information, or leading an academic discussion; he speaks firsthand, confronting people with the personal will of God.

What healing did Jesus refer to?

Lord Jesus, draw me out of the crowd of spectators into the band of disciples. I would not be among those who marvel and argue and discuss, but among those who listen and obey and believe. Amen.

September 14

I Am from Him

Now some of the people of Jerusalem were saying, "Is not this the man whom they are trying to kill? And here he is, speaking openly, but they say nothing to him! Can it be that the authorities really know that this is the Messiah? Yet we know where this man is from; but when the Messiah comes, no one will know where he is from." Then Jesus cried out as he was teaching in the temple, "You know me, and you know where I am from. I have not come on my own. But the one who sent me is true, and you do not know him. I know him, because I am from him, and he sent me." Then they tried to arrest him, but no one laid hands on him, because his hour had not yet come. Yet many in the crowd believed in him and were saying, "When the Messiah comes, will he do more signs than this man has done?"

JOHN 7:25–31

Jesus cannot be understood or explained in terms of his family life or his home-town origins. He can only be accounted for in terms of God's eternal plan of salvation and his gracious will to incarnation.

What signs had Jesus done?

Lead me deep into the sources of faith, O God. Take me beneath the surface so that I may see and understand the great and invisible foundation realities in your will and love. Amen.

September 15

What Does He Mean . . . ?

The Pharisees heard the crowd muttering such things about him, and the chief priests and Pharisees sent temple police to arrest him. Jesus then said, "I will be with you a little while longer, and then I am going to him who sent me. You will search for me, but you will not find me; and where I am, you cannot come." The Jews said to one another, "Where does this man intend to go that we will not find him? Does he intend to go to the Dispersion among the Greeks and teach the Greeks? What does he mean by saying, 'You will search for me and you will not find me" and "Where I am, you cannot come'?"

JOHN 7:32–36

Hostile opposition and skeptical rejection prevent understanding. Those who resist Jesus misunderstand Jesus. Faith, on the other hand, opens up the understanding, while obedience clarifies the revelation.

What was the "dispersion"?

I want a better understanding of your will for me, Lord; I want more light on your ways in my life. Direct me into the acts of obedience and the affirmations of faith that will show me what you are doing, in Jesus Christ. Amen.

September 16

Division in the Crowd

On the last day of the festival, the great day, while Jesus was standing there, he cried out, "Let anyone who is thirsty come to me, and let the one who believes in me drink. As the scripture has said, 'Out of the believer's heart shall flow rivers of living water.'" . . . When they heard these words, some in the crowd said, "This is really the prophet." Others said, "This is the Messiah." But some asked, "Surely the Messiah does not come from Galilee, does he? Has not the scripture said that the Messiah is descended from David and comes from Bethlehem, the village where David lived?" So there was a division in the crowd because of him. Some of them wanted to arrest him, but no one laid hands on him.

JOHN 7:37–44

In their disagreement they agreed on one thing: Jesus was highly significant. He was either the best they had met, bringing to completion all God's ways with them, or he was a most dangerous impostor, who would, if permitted, lead people astray from God. No one dismissed him as a trifle.

Do you take Jesus seriously?

Father, keep my attention on the center—on eternal matters of creation and salvation, on the great realities of grace and truth, on the concerns for forgiveness and reconciliation, on decisions of faith—on Christ, in whose name I pray. Amen.

September 17

Caught in the Very Act

The scribes and the Pharisees brought a woman who had been caught in adultery; and making her stand before all of them, they said to him, "Teacher, this woman was caught in the very act of committing adultery. Now in the law Moses commanded us to stone such women. Now what do you say?" . . . Jesus bent down and wrote with his finger on the ground. When they kept on questioning him, he straightened up and said to them, "Let anyone among you who is without sin be the first to throw a stone at her." And once again he bent down and wrote on the ground. When they heard it, they went away, one by one, beginning with the elders; and Jesus was left alone with the woman standing before him. Jesus straightened up and said to her, "Woman, where are they? Has no one condemned you?" She said, "No one, sir." And Jesus said, "Neither do I condemn you. Go your way, and from now on do not sin again."

JOHN 8:3–11

Jesus takes sin more seriously than anyone, but he responds to it differently than most. He does not condemn, rejecting the sinner; he does not condone, ignoring the sin; he forgives.

Compare this with Romans 8:1.

Released from the tyranny of condemnation—by critics and by conscience— I find all things new, O Lord. Instill now strong habits of virtue in place of the sins to which I had become accustomed. Amen.

September 18

I Am the Light of the World

Again Jesus spoke to them, saying, "I am the light of the world. Whoever follows me will never walk in darkness but will have the light of life."

JOHN 8:12

Light, God's creative work on the first day (Genesis 1:3), is basic: it warms and illuminates. Jesus is light in this original sense: the condition for beginning life and the energy for continuing life.

Compare this with John 1:1–9.

"O gladsome light, O grace of God the Father's face, th'eternal splendor wearing; celestial, holy, blest, our Saviour Jesus Christ, joyful in Thine appearing." * *Amen.*

* Ancient Greek hymn.

September 19

The Testimony of Two

Then the Pharisees said to him, "You are testifying on your own behalf; your testimony is not valid." Jesus answered, "Even if I testify on my own behalf, my testimony is valid because I know where I have come from and where I am going, but you do not know where I come from or where I am going. You judge by human standards; I judge no one. Yet even if I do judge, my judgment is valid; for it is not I alone who judge, but I and the Father who sent me. In your law it is written that the testimony of two witnesses is valid. I testify on my own behalf, and the Father who sent me testifies on my behalf."

JOHN 8:13–18

Jesus's critics were tangled up in questions of procedure, anxious over the technicalities of the messianic evidence. But these questions cannot be decided by courtroom cross-examination: on their knees, in prayer to the Father, they would have realized the truth of Jesus's words and acts.

Why all the hostility?

Father in heaven, I thank you for the convincing clarity of your Christ. Help me this day to pay attention to what is right before my eyes, and so learn your truth and receive by faith the gift of eternal life in Jesus Christ. Amen.

September 20

Where Is Your Father?

Then they said to him, "Where is your Father?" Jesus answered, "You know neither me nor my Father. If you knew me, you would know my Father also." He spoke these words while he was teaching in the treasury of the temple, but no one arrested him, because his hour had not yet come.

JOHN 8:19–20

Much religious talk is a form of unbelief. These Pharisees were not trying to discover the truth in Jesus. Their questions were not a quest for salvation. If they had been seriously interested in the location of the Father, they would have recognized his presence in Jesus.

Do you ever ask questions in order to avoid the truth?

Lord, use the questions I raise about you to lead me directly and quickly into your presence, for it is not answers about you that I want but fellowship with you, in and through Jesus Christ. Amen.

September 21

Who Are You?

Again he said to them, "I am going away, and you will search for me, but you will die in your sin. Where I am going, you cannot come." Then the Jews said, "Is he going to kill himself? Is that what he means by saying, 'Where I am going, you cannot come'?" . . . They said to him, "Who are you?" Jesus said to them, "Why do I speak to you at all? I have much to say about you and much to condemn; but the one who sent me is true, and I declare to the world what I have heard from him." They did not understand that he was speaking to them about the Father. So Jesus said, "When you have lifted up the Son of Man, then you will realize that I am he, and that I do nothing on my own, but I speak these things as the Father instructed me. And the one who sent me is with me; he has not left me alone, for I always do what is pleasing to him."

JOHN 8:21–29

Truth, the reality that is at the basis of all appearance, comes not so much by means of our intellect as through our obedience ("continue in my word") in personal relationship with Jesus. We find it not by reading books or by working in laboratories, but in following Jesus.

In what ways are you not free?

Free me, O Christ, from superstitions that confuse my mind, from misinformation that diverts me from obedience, from ignorance that pretends to be faith, so that I may run unfettered in the way of your commandments. Amen.

September 22

Free Indeed

"If you continue in my word, you are truly my disciples; and you will know the truth, and the truth will make you free." They answered him, "We are descendants of Abraham and have never been slaves to anyone. What do you mean by saying, 'You will be made free'?" Jesus answered them, "Very truly, I tell you, everyone who commits sin is a slave to sin. The slave does not have a permanent place in the household; the son has a place there forever. So if the Son makes you free, you will be free indeed. I know that you are descendants of Abraham; yet you look for an opportunity to kill me, because there is no place in you for my word. I declare what I have seen in the Father's presence; as for you, you should do what you have heard from the Father."

JOHN 8:31–38

Sin promises what it cannot deliver: it promises freedom, a life of self-will unencumbered by God's will; it promises a future, a life of fulfillment, where personal desires are indulged and satisfied. But the promises are lies. Only God can provide freedom and future for us.

Do you feel free?

"Make me a captive, Lord, and then I shall be free; force me to render up my sword, and I shall conqueror be." * Amen.

---

* George Matheson, "Make Me a Captive, Lord," *The Hymnbook*, 264.

September 23

The Father of Lies

They answered him, "Abraham is our father." Jesus said to them, "If you were Abraham's children, you would be doing what Abraham did, but now you are trying to kill me, a man who has told you the truth that I heard from God. This is not what Abraham did. You are indeed doing what your father does." They said to him, "We are not illegitimate children; we have one father, God himself." Jesus said to them, "If God were your Father, you would love me, for I came from God and now I am here. I did not come on my own, but he sent me. Why do you not understand what I say? It is because you cannot accept my word. You are from your father the devil, and you choose to do your father's desires. He was a murderer from the beginning and does not stand in the truth, because there is no truth in him. When he lies, he speaks according to his own nature, for he is a liar and the father of lies. But because I tell the truth, you do not believe me."

JOHN 8:39–45

All the original and true relationships—with Abraham as our father in faith, with God as our father in love—are distorted by sin. We need supernatural help from the very start to recognize and respond to the truth in Jesus Christ.

How is Abraham your father?

God, I will not rely on my own understanding or trust in my own good intentions: reveal your truth to me in Jesus and move me to faith by your Spirit, so that I may live truly and freely. Amen.

Why Do You Not Believe Me?

"Which of you convicts me of sin? If I tell the truth, why do you not believe me? Whoever is from God hears the words of God. The reason you do not hear them is that you are not from God."

JOHN 8:46–47

The act of unbelief is not, as so many seem to think, a matter of an overactive, skeptical intellect. It is a stubborn and irrational act of will—a refusal to be in relationship with God.

What grounds did the Jews have for their unbelief?

You have assembled all the materials in creation to show your purposes, O God. You have revealed your very heart of love in Jesus to convince me of your goodness. All truth witnesses to you and all goodness leads to you. Hallelujah! Amen.

September 25

My Father Who Glorifies

The Jews answered him, "Are we not right in saying that you are a Samaritan and have a demon?" Jesus answered, "I do not have a demon; but I honor my Father, and you dishonor me. Yet I do not seek my own glory; there is one who seeks it and he is the judge. Very truly, I tell you, whoever keeps my word will never see death." The Jews said to him, "Now we know that you have a demon. Abraham died, and so did the prophets; yet you say, 'Whoever keeps my word will never taste death.' Are you greater than our father Abraham, who died? The prophets also died. Who do you claim to be?" Jesus answered, "If I glorify myself, my glory is nothing. It is my Father who glorifies me, he of whom you say, 'He is our God,' though you do not know him. But I know him; if I would say that I do not know him, I would be a liar like you. But I do know him and I keep his word. Your ancestor Abraham rejoiced that he would see my day; he saw it and was glad." Then the Jews said to him, "You are not yet fifty years old, and have you seen Abraham?" Jesus said to them, "Very truly, I tell you, before Abraham was, I am." So they picked up stones to throw at him, but Jesus hid himself and went out of the temple.

JOHN 8:48–59

Jesus meets us, even when we are rude, where we are; but he will not cut down the garment of God's glory to fit our emaciated and underweight expectations: We are going to have to change, acquiring an appetite for a living God and a zest for eternity.

What don't you understand about Jesus?

Lord, I'm beginning to realize the way you work: you come to my level and attend to my difficulties so that I might come up to your level and share your glory. Thank you for your patience in starting with me where I am and your perseverance in taking me to where you are. Amen.

September 26

Who Sinned ...?

As he walked along, he saw a man blind from birth. His disciples asked him, "Rabbi, who sinned, this man or his parents, that he was born blind?" Jesus answered, "Neither this man nor his parents sinned; he was born blind so that God's works might be revealed in him. We must work the works of him who sent me while it is day; night is coming when no one can work. As long as I am in the world, I am the light of the world."

JOHN 9:1–5

Will we look on people in need—the ill and unfortunate—with accusing blame or with expectant hope? Are we interested in subjecting them to a moral dissection, or in holding them up to the light of God's glory?

Note the similarities with John 1:4 and 8:12.

Lord Jesus, root out from my spirit the morbid curiosity that wants to pry into all the details of my neighbors' troubles, and replace it with a zestful interest in the glorious ways that you save and heal. Amen.

September 27

The Pool of Siloam

When he had said this, he spat on the ground and made mud with the saliva and spread the mud on the man's eyes, saying to him, "Go, wash in the pool of Siloam" (which means Sent). Then he went and washed and came back able to see. . . . They brought to the Pharisees the man who had formerly been blind. Now it was a sabbath day when Jesus made the mud and opened his eyes. Then the Pharisees also began to ask him how he had received his sight. He said to them, "He put mud on my eyes. Then I washed, and now I see." Some of the Pharisees said, "This man is not from God, for he does not observe the sabbath." But others said, "How can a man who is a sinner perform such signs?" And they were divided. So they said again to the blind man, "What do you say about him? It was your eyes he opened." He said, "He is a prophet." The Jews did not believe that he had been blind and had received his sight until they called the parents of the man who had received his sight and asked them, "Is this your son, who you say was born blind? How then does he now see?" His parents answered, "We know that this is our son, and that he was born blind; but we do not know how it is that now he sees, nor do we know who opened his eyes. Ask him; he is of age. He will speak for himself." His parents said this because they were afraid of the Jews; for the Jews had already agreed that anyone who confessed Jesus to be the Messiah would be put out of the synagogue. Therefore his parents said, "He is of age; ask him." So for the second time they called the man who had been blind, and they said to him, "Give glory to God! We know that this man is a sinner." He answered, "I do not know whether he is a sinner. One thing I do know, that though I was blind, now I see." They said to him, "What did he do to you? How did he open your eyes?" He answered them, "I have told you already, and you would not listen. Why do you want to hear it again? Do you also want to become his disciples?" Then they reviled him, saying, "You are his disciple, but we are disciples of Moses. We know that God has spoken to Moses, but as for this man, we do not know where he comes from." The man answered, "Here is an astonishing thing! You do not know where he comes from, and yet he opened my eyes. We know that God does not listen to sinners, but he does listen to one who worships him and obeys his will. Never since the world began has it been heard that anyone opened the eyes of a person born blind. If this man were not from God, he could do nothing." They answered him, "You were born entirely in sins, and are you trying to teach us?" And they drove him out.

JOHN 9:6–34

In obeying the directions of Jesus, the man experienced the light of Jesus. "All right knowledge of God is born of obedience."* Jesus is not a theory about light, he is light whom we experience by submitting to his touch and responding to his commands.

Do you know where the pool of Siloam is?

Touch me, command me, send me, Lord Jesus. Lead me out of the long night of my sin into the bright day of your salvation. I would live in your light and by your light. Amen.

* Calvin, *Institutes of the Christian Religion*, vol. 1 (Philadelphia, PA: Westminster Press, 1960), 72.

September 28

And He Worshiped Him

Jesus heard that they had driven him out, and when he found him, he
said, "Do you believe in the Son of Man?" He answered, "And who is
he, sir? Tell me, so that I may believe in him." Jesus said to him, "You
have seen him, and the one speaking with you is he." He said, "Lord,
I believe." And he worshiped him.

JOHN 9:35–38

Excommunicated from the synagogue because of Christ, the
man is now drawn into deep communion with God through
Christ. His belief was not an item of information to which he gave
assent, but a personal relationship to which he made a courageous
commitment.

What is the relation between belief and worship?

*I thank you, dear heavenly Father, for the work of Jesus: for the light he
sheds on my way; for the ability he gives me to see the next step. As I
follow in faith, lead me step by step into your fullness. Amen.*

September 29

We Are Not Blind . . . ?

Jesus said, "I came into this world for judgment so that those who do not see may see, and those who do see may become blind." Some of the Pharisees near him heard this and said to him, "Surely we are not blind, are we?" Jesus said to them, "If you were blind, you would not have sin. But now that you say, 'We see,' your sin remains."

JOHN 9:39–41

Jesus is the light: in his presence even the worst instance of blindness (the man born blind) is able to see; apart from his presence even the best instance of enlightenment (the Pharisee) cannot see a thing.

How were the Pharisees blind?

"O God of Light, Thy Word, a lamp unfailing, shines through the darkness of our earthly ways, o'er fear and doubt, o'er black despair prevailing, guiding our steps to Thine eternal day." * Amen.

---

* Sarah E. Taylor, "O God of Light, Thy Word, a Lamp Unfailing," *The Hymnbook,* 217.

September 30

A Thief and a Bandit

"Very truly, I tell you, anyone who does not enter the sheepfold by the gate but climbs in by another way is a thief and a bandit. The one who enters by the gate is the shepherd of the sheep. The gatekeeper opens the gate for him, and the sheep hear his voice. He calls his own sheep by name and leads them out."

JOHN 10:1–3

There is an immense amount of theft and violence in religion. Certain unscrupulous people, making concern for souls a pretext, pose as messengers of God but treat people as plunder, using them to get rich or to become powerful.

Have you ever been misled by a religious leader?

You have instructed me, Lord, to "test the spirits": sharpen my awareness of truth. Give me wisdom to discern the falsehood that hides behind poses of piety and the mendacity that dresses in a cloak of religion. Amen.

October 1

They Know His Voice

"When he has brought out all his own, he goes ahead of them, and the sheep follow him because they know his voice. They will not follow a stranger, but they will run from him because they do not know the voice of strangers." Jesus used this figure of speech with them, but they did not understand what he was saying to them.

JOHN 10:4–6

Just as sheep are familiar with the voice of their shepherd, so Christians are familiar with the voice of their Lord. Long association in a covenant of love substantiates faithfulness.

Read Psalm 23 for background.

In gratitude I listen to and obey your voice, Lord Jesus. Call me into paths of compassion and service, into ways of praise and joy, into places of hope and adoration. Amen.

October 2

I Am the Gate

So again Jesus said to them, "Very truly, I tell you, I am the gate for the sheep. All who came before me are thieves and bandits; but the sheep did not listen to them. I am the gate. Whoever enters by me will be saved, and will come in and go out and find pasture."

JOHN 10:7–9

Jesus is a passageway. Going one way he leads us into the external world of creation, the visible realities of all things made in love and with purpose. Going the other way he leads us into the internal world of redemption, the invisible realities of grace and mercy which hold all things together.

What are some other functions of a door?

Through you, Lord Jesus Christ, I find my way out into a grand creation where everything is evidence of the Father's majesty; and find my way into the word where all is sustained and alive by the Spirit. Thank you for clear and easy access both ways. Amen.

October 3

Abundantly

"The thief comes only to steal and kill and destroy. I came that they may have life, and have it abundantly."

JOHN 10:10

Jesus does not need us to complete inadequacies in himself. He has no need to plunder our already depleted resources. He is already whole—and more: he overflows with life in himself and therefore is able to give to us, not take from us; to complete us, not exploit us.

What more do you want from God?

Fearlessly and hopefully I receive you, O Christ: show me what I must do to live in health; lead me to the places where I live with meaning; provide me with the strength in which I can live exuberantly. Amen.

October 4

<hr>

Good Shepherd

"I am the good shepherd. The good shepherd lays down his life for the sheep."

JOHN 10:11

A persistent and influential image for God in scripture is "shepherd." By it we understand God in Christ as strong and tender, courageous and intimate, provident and personal.

Read Ezekiel 34:7–16.

"The King of love my Shepherd is, whose goodness faileth never; I nothing lack if I am His and He is mine forever. In death's dark vale I fear no ill with Thee, dear Lord, beside me; Thy rod and staff my comfort still, Thy cross before to guide me." * Amen.

---

* Henry W. Baker, "The King of Love My Shepherd Is," *The Hymnbook*, 100.

October 5

The Hired Hand

"The hired hand, who is not the shepherd and does not own the sheep, sees the wolf coming and leaves the sheep and runs away—and the wolf snatches them and scatters them. The hired hand runs away because a hired hand does not care for the sheep."

JOHN 10:12–13

There is nothing worse than people who use the spiritual needs of others to serve their own pride, who pretend to care for souls but only care for themselves. Jesus, in contrast, is unique and noble: completely without self-interest, wholly attendant on our eternal well-being.

What is a "hired hand"?

Father, how I thank you for sending Jesus to be my shepherd: a Lord whom I can trust completely without the fear of being misled, a Savior upon whom I can rely absolutely, without the anxiety of being abandoned. Amen.

One Flock, One Shepherd

"I am the good shepherd. I know my own and my own know me, just as the Father knows me and I know the Father. And I lay down my life for the sheep. I have other sheep that do not belong to this fold. I must bring them also, and they will listen to my voice. So there will be one flock, one shepherd."

JOHN 10:14–16

A good shepherd does not play favorites, concentrating his attention on a few and ignoring the many. The shepherd's concern and affection far exceed what a single fold of sheep, or a particular sheep, can experience or even be aware of.

Who are some of the "other sheep"?

Shepherd Christ, I hear your voice; how many others hear it too? As you lead me into green pastures and beside still waters, guide me into a fellowship of love with others who follow you. Amen.

October 7

I Lay Down My Life

"For this reason the Father loves me, because I lay down my life in order to take it up again. No one takes it from me, but I lay it down of my own accord. I have power to lay it down, and I have power to take it up again. I have received this command from my Father."

John 10:17–18

Jesus picks up an earlier statement (v. 11) and expands it: his shepherding is voluntary and it is sacrificial. He is not a puppet pulled by the strings of fate: he chooses. And he is not a victim overwhelmed by malign forces: his sacrifice will conclude in a resurrection.

How did Jesus "lay down" his life?

Thank you, Lord Jesus, for going all the way for me, to the cross and to death, making there a "full, perfect, and sufficient sacrifice for the sins of the world" and for my sins. Amen.

October 8

Tell Us Plainly

Many of them were saying, "He has a demon and is out of his mind. Why listen to him?" Others were saying, "These are not the words of one who has a demon. Can a demon open the eyes of the blind?" At that time the festival of the Dedication took place in Jerusalem. . . . So the Jews gathered around him and said to him, "How long will you keep us in suspense? If you are the Messiah, tell us plainly." Jesus answered, "I have told you, and you do not believe. The works that I do in my Father's name testify to me; but you do not believe, because you do not belong to my sheep. My sheep hear my voice. I know them, and they follow me. I give them eternal life, and they will never perish. No one will snatch them out of my hand."

JOHN 10:20–28

Those who insist on playing the leading part on center stage, using God only as background scenery and permitting him only a few off-stage whispers, will also complain that he does not speak clearly or act plainly. Of course not. But the fault is in their pride, not in his revelation.

What do you know about the Feast of Dedication?

Lord, when others suggest detours through cloud-shadowed lanes of skepticism, direct me into the sunlit clarity of faith so that I may walk in your ways and not stumble, advance in your will and not wander, and come, finally, to your presence, where I will know even as I am known. Amen.

October 9

Out of the Father's Hand

"What my Father has given me is greater than all else, and no one can snatch it out of the Father's hand. The Father and I are one."

JOHN 10:29–30

Through Jesus we discover, by faith, absolute trust: that which we turn over to God is secure. He is not careless or absentminded with the precious treasure of our lives. God takes care of that which we give him.

What have you entrusted into the Father's hand?

I commit myself and those I live with into your safekeeping, dear Father. Permit no evil to ruin our faith, no testing to damage our obedience, no unbelief to diminish our love, no anxieties to weaken our hope. You bought us with a great price; now keep us for eternity. Amen.

October 10

Blasphemy

The Jews took up stones again to stone him. Jesus replied, "I have shown you many good works from the Father. For which of these are you going to stone me?" The Jews answered, "It is not for a good work that we are going to stone you, but for blasphemy, because you, though only a human being, are making yourself God."

JOHN 10:31–33

Jesus's opponents were quite clear about one thing: Jesus was not merely a nice man running good-natured errands for the neighbors. He was either the very God or a blasphemer. Their accusation, while wrong, at least showed that they understood the issue.

Read Leviticus 24:16 for background.

Eternal God, I thank you for the mystery and miracle of your presence in Christ. You reveal yourself truly and share yourself wholly. Praise be to you, Father, Son, and Holy Spirit. Amen.

October 11

Believe the Works

Jesus answered, "Is it not written in your law, 'I said, you are gods'? If those to whom the word of God came were called 'gods'—and the scripture cannot be annulled—can you say that the one whom the Father has sanctified and sent into the world is blaspheming because I said, 'I am God's Son'? If I am not doing the works of my Father, then do not believe me. But if I do them, even though you do not believe me, believe the works, so that you may know and understand that the Father is in me and I am in the Father." Then they tried to arrest him again, but he escaped from their hands. He went away again across the Jordan to the place where John had been baptizing earlier, and he remained there. Many came to him, and they were saying, "John performed no sign, but everything that John said about this man was true." And many believed in him there.

JOHN 10:34–42

Jesus didn't say one thing and do another; he did what he said and said what he did. We can begin with either form of the revelation—the verbal or the visible, the words or the works—and be led to the same conclusion: this is the Christ of God.

God, thank you for giving me the whole picture in Jesus. Take everything I see and everything I hear and arrange it into a coherent, convincing revelation of your will to salvation. Amen.

Lazarus ... Is Ill

Now a certain man was ill, Lazarus of Bethany, the village of Mary and her sister Martha. Mary was the one who anointed the Lord with perfume and wiped his feet with her hair; her brother Lazarus was ill. So the sisters sent a message to Jesus, "Lord, he whom you love is ill." But when Jesus heard it, he said, "This illness does not lead to death; rather it is for God's glory, so that the Son of God may be glorified through it."

JOHN 11:1–4

No misfortune, it seems, is a disaster. Nothing is able, in itself, to separate us from God's purposes in Christ. And so Jesus's response to Lazarus' illness is both casual and confident. Even the things we call evil can be used by God to demonstrate his glory.

Why did the sisters send for Jesus?

You know, Lord, how faithless and nervous I am in the presence of illness and death: even though I know you are the great Physician; even though I know you are the resurrection and the life. Teach me to live in hope, responsive every moment to your glory. Amen.

October 13

Lazarus Is Dead

Accordingly, though Jesus loved Martha and her sister and Lazarus, after having heard that Lazarus was ill, he stayed two days longer in the place where he was. Then after this he said to the disciples, "Let us go to Judea again." The disciples said to him, "Rabbi, the Jews were just now trying to stone you, and are you going there again?" Jesus answered, '"Are there not twelve hours of daylight? Those who walk during the day do not stumble, because they see the light of this world. But those who walk at night stumble, because the light is not in them." . . . Then Jesus told them plainly, "Lazarus is dead. For your sake I am glad I was not there, so that you may believe. But let us go to him." Thomas, who was called the Twin, said to his fellow disciples, "Let us also go, that we may die with him."

JOHN 11:5–16

Christ's love does not operate in the grooves of our expectation: he does not rush to heal Lazarus; he does not hurry to comfort Mary and Martha. But his measured, deliberate pace leads to an action that far exceeds our expectations.

Why did Jesus delay his coming?

"Unresting, unhasting, and silent as light, nor wanting, nor wasting, Thou rulest in might; Thy justice like mountains high soaring above, Thy clouds which are fountains of goodness and love." * Amen.

* Walter Chalmers Smith, "Immortal, Invisible, God Only Wise," *The Hymnbook*, 82.

October 14

I Am the Resurrection

When Jesus arrived, he found that Lazarus had already been in the tomb four days. Now Bethany was near Jerusalem, some two miles away, and many of the Jews had come to Martha and Mary to console them about their brother. When Martha heard that Jesus was coming, she went and met him, while Mary stayed at home. Martha said to Jesus, "Lord, if you had been here, my brother would not have died. But even now I know that God will give you whatever you ask of him." Jesus said to her, "Your brother will rise again." Martha said to him, "I know that he will rise again in the resurrection on the last day." Jesus said to her, "I am the resurrection and the life. Those who believe in me, even though they die, will live, and everyone who lives and believes in me will never die. Do you believe this?" She said to him, "Yes, Lord, I believe that you are the Messiah, the Son of God, the one coming into the world."

JOHN 11:17–27

In Christ our destiny is not dissolution or annihilation or transmigration—or any of the other possibilities guessed by restless and curious minds—but actual, historical resurrection.

What is resurrection?

I believe in your resurrection, Lord Jesus Christ, and praise your marvelous and mighty name; and I believe in my resurrection, and wonder at your compassion and concern. You have the last word, and the last word is life, not death. Amen.

October 15

Jesus Began to Weep

[Martha] went back and called her sister Mary, and told her privately, "The Teacher is here and is calling for you." And when she heard it, she got up quickly and went to him. . . . The Jews who were with her in the house, consoling her, saw Mary get up quickly and go out. They followed her because they thought that she was going to the tomb to weep there. When Mary came where Jesus was and saw him, she knelt at his feet and said to him, "Lord, if you had been here, my brother would not have died." When Jesus saw her weeping, and the Jews who came with her also weeping, he was greatly disturbed in spirit and deeply moved. He said, "Where have you laid him?" They said to him, "Lord, come and see." Jesus began to weep. So the Jews said, "See how he loved him!" But some of them said, "Could not he who opened the eyes of the blind man have kept this man from dying?"

JOHN 11:28–37

The power of Jesus did not isolate him from human pain or protect him from personal anguish. He participated in the emotions of death and grief completely. It is as important to realize his humanity ("Jesus wept") as it is to believe in his divinity ("I am the resurrection") if we are to respond to the complete Christ.

Why did Jesus weep?

Since, Lord, nothing I experience is foreign to you and nothing I feel is strange to you, I am bold to draw near to the throne of grace to receive mercy and find grace in time of need (Hebrews 4:16). Amen.

October 16

Lazarus, Come Out

Then Jesus, again greatly disturbed, came to the tomb. It was a cave, and a stone was lying against it. Jesus said, "Take away the stone." Martha, the sister of the dead man, said to him, "Lord, already there is a stench because he has been dead four days." Jesus said to her, "Did I not tell you that if you believed, you would see the glory of God?" So they took away the stone. And Jesus looked upward and said, "Father, I thank you for having heard me. I knew that you always hear me, but I have said this for the sake of the crowd standing here, so that they may believe that you sent me." When he had said this, he cried with a loud voice, "Lazarus, come out!" The dead man came out, his hands and feet bound with strips of cloth, and his face wrapped in a cloth. Jesus said to them, "Unbind him, and let him go."

JOHN 11:38–44

The same commanding word that penetrated chaos and brought heaven and earth into being, reached into the corruption of the grave and brought out a resurrection life.

What does this passage mean to you?

"I have a grave of sin. . . . Where Lazarus had been four days, I have been for fifty years. Why dost Thou not call me, as Thou didst him? I need Thy thunder, O my God! Thy music will not serve me."* Amen.

* John Donne, *Devotions upon Emergent Occasions* (Ann Arbor: University of Michigan Press, 1959), 141.

October 17

Filled with the Fragrance

Six days before the Passover Jesus came to Bethany, the home of Lazarus, whom he had raised from the dead. There they gave a dinner for him. Martha served, and Lazarus was one of those at the table with him. Mary took a pound of costly perfume made of pure nard, anointed Jesus's feet, and wiped them with her hair. The house was filled with the fragrance of the perfume. But Judas Iscariot, one of his disciples (the one who was about to betray him), said, "Why was this perfume not sold for three hundred denarii and the money given to the poor?" (He said this not because he cared about the poor, but because he was a thief; he kept the common purse and used to steal what was put into it.) Jesus said, "Leave her alone. She bought it so that she might keep it for the day of my burial. You always have the poor with you, but you do not always have me."

JOHN 12:1–8

The generous gift of Mary and the stingy complaint of Judas are placed in contrast. Mary used what she had to adore Jesus; Judas used Jesus to enrich himself. Mary is led into a life of devotion that is beautiful; Judas is posted as a warning against letting money get between us and God.

What are some other contrasts between Mary and Judas?

Lord, I place what I have in offering to you. And not just my money, but my life—my energies, my abilities and my goals. Let everything be fragrant in devotion to you. Amen.

October 18

A Grain of Wheat

[The crowd] heard that Jesus was coming to Jerusalem. So they took branches of palm trees and went out to meet him, shouting, "Hosanna! Blessed is the one who comes in the name of the Lord— the King of Israel!" . . . Now among those who went up to worship at the festival were some Greeks. They came to Philip, . . . and said to him, "Sir, we wish to see Jesus." Philip went and told Andrew; then Andrew and Philip went and told Jesus. Jesus answered them, "The hour has come for the Son of Man to be glorified. Very truly, I tell you, unless a grain of wheat falls into the earth and dies, it remains just a single grain; but if it dies, it bears much fruit. Those who love their life lose it, and those who hate their life in this world will keep it for eternal life. Whoever serves me must follow me, and where I am, there will my servant be also. Whoever serves me, the Father will honor."

JOHN 12:12–26

Jesus demonstrated, in word and act, how our lives are seed to be planted, not fruit to be preserved. When we realize the centrality of God in our lives, we are able to understand ourselves as gifts that we are free to share, rather than as possessions that we must anxiously protect.

How did Jesus demonstrate this saying?

Where do I plant myself today, Lord? in what acts of love? in what routines of service? In what words of witness? I wait for your direction, ready to follow your lead. Amen.

October 19

This Voice

"Now my soul is troubled. And what should I say—'Father, save me from this hour'? No, it is for this reason that I have come to this hour. Father, glorify your name." Then a voice came from heaven, "I have glorified it, and I will glorify it again." The crowd standing there heard it and said that it was thunder. Others said, "An angel has spoken to him." Jesus answered, "This voice has come for your sake, not for mine. Now is the judgment of this world; now the ruler of this world will be driven out. And I, when I am lifted up from the earth, will draw all people to myself. . . . The light is with you for a little longer. Walk while you have the light, so that the darkness may not overtake you. If you walk in the darkness, you do not know where you are going. While you have the light, believe in the light, so that you may become children of light."

JOHN 12:27–36

It is all important that we realize the essential relation between Father and Son, between the heavenly voice and the earthly ministry, between the glorious will and purpose of God and the act of glory that is the death and resurrection of Jesus.

Compare this with Daniel 7:13–14.

Your acts are light, Lord Jesus, and your words are light—candescent marks that show the path of pilgrimage to God. Keep my eyes open to what you reveal and my heart obedient to what you will. Amen.

October 20

. . . But to Save the World

Although he had performed so many signs in their presence, they did not believe in him. . . . Then Jesus cried aloud: "Whoever believes in me believes not in me but in him who sent me. And whoever sees me sees him who sent me. I have come as light into the world, so that everyone who believes in me should not remain in the darkness. I do not judge anyone who hears my words and does not keep them, for I came not to judge the world, but to save the world. The one who rejects me and does not receive my word has a judge; on the last day the word that I have spoken will serve as judge, for I have not spoken on my own, but the Father who sent me has himself given me a commandment about what to say and what to speak. And I know that his commandment is eternal life. What I speak, therefore, I speak just as the Father has told me."

JOHN 12:37–50

Jesus makes a last, vigorous attempt to persuade the crowds—to break through the indifference of some and the fear of others. He is passionate and single-minded in his ministry of revealing God's will, drawing people to salvation and commanding eternal life.

How does judgment get set in motion?

Save me, Lord Jesus Christ: expose my sin and lead me to the place of forgiveness. Heal my faithlessness and make me healthy with love; convert my rebellion and train me in persevering discipleship. Amen.

October 21

Are You Going to Wash My Feet?

Now before the festival of the Passover, Jesus knew that his hour had come to depart from this world and go to the Father. Having loved his own who were in the world, he loved them to the end. The devil had already put it into the heart of Judas son of Simon Iscariot to betray him. And during supper Jesus, knowing that the Father had given all things into his hands, and that he had come from God and was going to God, got up from the table, took off his outer robe, and tied a towel around himself. Then he poured water into a basin and began to wash the disciples' feet and to wipe them with the towel that was tied around him. He came to Simon Peter, who said to him, "Lord, are you going to wash my feet?" Jesus answered, "You do not know now what I am doing, but later you will understand."

JOHN 13:1–7

For some people, accepting an act of ministry is more difficult than offering it, for when another assists us our dependence, weakness, and need are admitted. When Peter abandons his pose as the all-sufficient self-made man and receives Jesus's ministry, he acts by faith.

Is it difficult for you to accept help?

I know, Lord, that it is pride that wants to assert absolute independence and be free from all obligations. I would like never to have to ask anybody for anything, not even you. Forgive my self-righteousness and clothe me in your righteousness. Amen.

October 22

Entirely Clean

Peter said to him, "You will never wash my feet." Jesus answered, "Unless I wash you, you have no share with me." Simon Peter said to him, "Lord, not my feet only but also my hands and my head!"

John 13:8–9

The acts of ministry that impinge upon us in Christ are not tokens, external trivialities that may or may not remind us of something important; they are sacr*Amen*tal signs: evidence of a deep and thoroughgoing inward transformation.

Compare this with 1 John 1:9.

Cleanse me, Christ. Wash the stain of sin from my soul, blow the dust of doubt from my mind, wipe the dirt of evil from my spirit: "I long to be perfectly whole." Amen.

October 23

Not All of You Are Clean

Jesus said to him, "One who has bathed does not need to wash, except for the feet, but is entirely clean. And you are clean, though not all of you." For he knew who was to betray him; for this reason he said, "Not all of you are clean."

JOHN 13:10–11

Judas submitted his feet to Jesus's washing, but withheld his heart. The water never got beneath his skin. Christ's cleansing requires inner acceptance.

Why did Judas betray Jesus?

"Have mercy on me, O God, according to Thy steadfast love; according to Thy abundant mercy blot out my transgressions. Wash me thoroughly from my iniquity, and cleanse me from my sin!" (Psalm 51:1–2). Amen.

October 24

An Example

After he had washed their feet, had put on his robe, and had returned to the table, he said to them, "Do you know what I have done to you? You call me Teacher and Lord—and you are right, for that is what I am. So if I, your Lord and Teacher, have washed your feet, you also ought to wash one another's feet. For I have set you an example, that you also should do as I have done to you."

JOHN 13:12–15

Jesus's life is not only a unique and indispensable ministry—the one we need to reveal God to us and to reconcile us to God—but our common example, the model from which we learn to live truly and rightly.

What act of service will you do today?

Lord Jesus, you couldn't have made it any more clear; you couldn't have said it more plainly. Why do I have so much difficulty following your example?—pride gets in the way. Overcome my selfishness and train me in devout service. Amen.

You Are Blessed

"Very truly, I tell you, servants are not greater than their master, nor are messengers greater than the one who sent them. If you know these things, you are blessed if you do them."

JOHN 13:16–17

Knowing is not enough. Understanding must be completed by obedience. What the head knows and the heart feels must be coordinated with what the hands do and where the feet go.

How do you express your faith in action?

Servant Christ, you show me how to serve; you command me to serve; you bless me as I serve. I praise you for the servant way, its joy and its glory. Amen.

October 26

You May Believe

"I am not speaking of all of you; I know whom I have chosen. But it is to fulfill the scripture, 'The one who ate my bread has lifted his heel against me.' I tell you this now, before it occurs, so that when it does occur, you may believe that I am he."

JOHN 13:18–19

The way Jesus will turn Judas 'betrayal, the Jewish trial, and the Roman crucifixion into an act of atonement and redemption is as powerful an incentive to belief as the positive acts of revelation in which he showed his glory.

What scripture does Jesus quote?

Even more impressive, Lord, than the signs that show your life and your love is the way you use the malice of evil men to do the work of salvation: "Surely the wrath of men shall praise thee!" Amen.

October 27

Receives

"Very truly, I tell you, whoever receives one whom I send receives me; and whoever receives me receives him who sent me."

JOHN 13:20

We take what God gives through the servant whom he sends. The act of ministry is for our salvation whether or not the minister is to our taste. We cannot be snobbish; we must not be fussy. Receive.

Whom has God sent to you?

Father, you send messengers and provide ministries; and I receive. Help me to be hospitable and open to all who come, grateful and accepting of each who speaks in your name, for "some have entertained angels unawares" (Hebrews 13:1). Amen.

October 28

Who Is It?

After saying this Jesus was troubled in spirit, and declared, "Very truly, I tell you, one of you will betray me." The disciples looked at one another, uncertain of whom he was speaking. One of his disciples—the one whom Jesus loved—was reclining next to him; Simon Peter therefore motioned to him to ask Jesus of whom he was speaking. So while reclining next to Jesus, he asked him, "Lord, who is it?" Jesus answered, "It is the one to whom I give this piece of bread when I have dipped it in the dish." So when he had dipped the piece of bread, he gave it to Judas son of Simon Iscariot. After he received the piece of bread, Satan entered into him. Jesus said to him, "Do quickly what you are going to do." ... So, after receiving the piece of bread, he immediately went out. And it was night.

JOHN 13:21–30

How a person who had been at Jesus's side for so long, who had experienced his virtue and enjoyed his blessing, could deliberately plot his betrayal escapes logic. All, though, who are not self-deceived know their own capacity for the entire range of sin.

Who was the disciple "whom Jesus loved?"

"O break, O break, hard heart of mine! Thy weak self-love and guilty pride His Pilate and His Judas were: Jesus our Lord, is crucified!" * Amen.

* F. W. Faber.

October 29

Glorified

When he had gone out, Jesus said, "Now the Son of Man has been glorified, and God has been glorified in him. If God has been glorified in him, God will also glorify him in himself and will glorify him at once."

JOHN 13:31–32

Glory—an important word in John's gospel—refers to the open display of God's good will, his loving salvation, his redeeming purpose. As Judas is swallowed up in the night, Jesus emphasizes this theme to focus attention on what God is doing, not on what Judas does.

How many times is glory mentioned here?

You know, God, my fondness for eavesdropping on the gossip of the wicked and entertaining in my heart tales of sin, when I should be absorbed in the dramatic story of salvation in Jesus. Help me to pay attention to what is really important—your works and your words. Amen.

October 30

A New Commandment

"I give you a new commandment, that you love one another. Just as I have loved you, you also should love one another."

JOHN 13:34

Love is defined ("as I have loved you") and commanded. It has nothing to do with soupy feelings, and it is not an optional feature for attachment to basic religion if we happen to be inclined in that direction. It is what Christ did and what we must do.

What is new about love?

Jesus Christ: your words have been flattened by so many repetitions and dulled by so many hypocrisies that I hear them as neither new nor commanding. By your Spirit restore fresh, explosive force to the words so that I may hear with zest and obey with zeal. Amen.

By This . . .

"By this everyone will know that you are my disciples, if you have love for one another."

JOHN 13:35

A most surprising identification card! Not "if we hold the right doctrine"; not "if we have membership in the right church"; not "if we work hard for justice"; not "if we are knowledgeable in scripture"; not "if we diligently and successfully use our talents." The only Christ-authorized mark of discipleship is love for one another.

Is this the way others recognize you?

Dear Jesus, you have showed me how to love you; you have commanded me to love; you are in and with me to love. Develop in me a deep, consistent and mature love for others. Amen.

November 1

Denied Me

Simon Peter said to him, "Lord, where are you going?" Jesus answered, "Where I am going, you cannot follow me now; but you will follow afterward." Peter said to him, "Lord, why can I not follow you now? I will lay down my life for you." Jesus answered, "Will you lay down your life for me? Very truly, I tell you, before the cock crows, you will have denied me three times."

JOHN 13:36–38

Among the twelve, Peter and Judas are the conspicuous sinners. But the contrasts between them are substantial: Judas's betrayal is calculated; Peter's denial is spontaneous. Judas's sin plunged him into the despair of outer darkness; Peter's sin brought him to a godly sorrow that worked repentance. No sin must separate us from God; any sin can.

In what other ways do Judas and Peter differ?

Father in heaven, I make many naive promises and brave-sounding resolves. Much of it is sounding brass and clashing cymbals. I start out expecting your congratulations and end up needing your compassion. Receive me in mercy and forgive me for the sake of Jesus Christ. Amen.

November 2

Believe

"Do not let your hearts be troubled. Believe in God, believe also in me."

John 14:1

The evening before his crucifixion, Jesus had an extended conversation with his disciples (John 14–17). His purpose was to prepare them for a courageous act of belief—to believe in him even when it looked like everything was falling apart.

What troubles do you face?

God, you well know how the troubles in the world and the troubles in my heart gang up on me and threaten to defeat me. I reaffirm my belief in your strong presence and wait on you to renew my strength, through Jesus Christ. Amen.

November 3

In My Father's House

"In my Father's house there are many dwelling places. If it were not so, would I have told you that I go to prepare a place for you? And if I go and prepare a place for you, I will come again and will take you to myself, so that where I am, there you may be also. And you know the way to the place where I am going."

JOHN 14:2–4

Heaven will not be a vast spectacular country to visit as a tourist; it is a place where we will have a home and dwell as citizens. Jesus's words make heaven as specific and sure as any dwelling place we know on earth.

Why is heaven important?

Lord Jesus, when I worry about the future, harboring anxieties about health or money or family, revive these words in my memory and refresh me with the knowledge that the future is where you are getting things ready for me. Amen.

November 4

. . . Can We Know the Way?

Thomas said to him, "Lord, we do not know where you are going. How can we know the way?" Jesus said to him, "I am the way, and the truth, and the life. No one comes to the Father except through me. If you know me, you will know my Father also. From now on you do know him and have seen him."

JOHN 14:5–7

Thomas's question defines our quest; Jesus's answer maps out our journey. But Jesus does more than give us a map. He not only plainly and personally shows us the way to God, he actually takes us to him.

Why is Jesus important?

Christ my Savior, how much motion I waste, how much needless searching I do, when all I have to do is follow you, listen to you, and let you live your eternal life in me: "I will run in the way of thy commandments when thou enlargest my understanding" (Psalm 119:32). Amen.

November 5

Show Us the Father

Philip said to him, "Lord, show us the Father, and we will be satisfied." Jesus said to him, "Have I been with you all this time, Philip, and you still do not know me? Whoever has seen me has seen the Father. How can you say, 'Show us the Father'? Do you not believe that I am in the Father and the Father is in me? The words that I say to you I do not speak on my own; but the Father who dwells in me does his works."

JOHN 14:8–10

Philip's question is a search for God; Jesus's answer ends the search: God is in Christ. God is historically revealed and defined. Speculations about God are over. Now the question is, "Will you believe in him, or not?"

What is your question?

Sometimes, Lord, I ask questions just to put off going to work as your disciple. I wonder if Philip was doing that? Like him, I know more than enough already—help me to put it into practice in active faith in Jesus Christ, your Son, my Savior. Amen.

November 6

Words. . . . Works

"Believe me that I am in the Father and the Father is in me; but if you do not, then believe me because of the works themselves."

JOHN 14:11

We can take the meaning of Jesus's words or we can observe the evidence of his works. We can listen to him or we can watch him. Both the words and the works lead to the same conclusion: Jesus reveals God to us.

Lord Jesus Christ, I thank you for your words—clear and convincing; and I thank you for your works—plain and definitive. Thank you for a complete revelation and a whole salvation. Amen.

November 7

Greater Works

"Very truly, I tell you, the one who believes in me will also do the works that I do and, in fact, will do greater works than these, because I am going to the Father."

JOHN 14:12

God does not want us to be docile followers of Jesus, so overawed by him that we never attempt anything but pale imitations of his works. He intends people full of initiative, expanding in countless ways the ministry of redemptive love he launched.

What are some of the "greater works"?

Father in heaven, it is hard for me to think of doing greater works than your Son. What those works are is your business; the willingness to shed my lazy timidity and start believing and praying after the manner of Jesus is mine, in whose name I ask for help to do it faithfully. Amen.

Ask

"I will do whatever you ask in my name, so that the Father may be glorified in the Son. If in my name you ask me for anything, I will do it."

JOHN 14:13–14

Too often we ask for things we don't need from people who can't supply our needs. Jesus's generous invitation, "Ask," involves us in receiving the gifts God has for us, in doing ministries to which he calls us, and experiencing the grace and mercy by which he completes us.

What will you ask God for?

God, instead of asking for many things I'll never need, from merchants and entertainers and friends, I will ask you for the few things I need eternally—light to take the next step in faith, grace to persevere for another day, forgiveness that changes sin to salvation. Amen.

If

"If you love me, you will keep my commandments."

JOHN 14:15

Obedience is rooted in love, not fear; it is activated by affection, not by force. Keeping the commandments, for Christians, is not dull rule-keeping but passionate love-making: each commandment is a channel for expressing and sharing God's goodness.

What are your favorite commandments?

Thank you for the commandments, God; for so many clear-cut and convenient ways to express my love for you and for others. "Seven times a day I praise thee for thy righteous ordinances!" (Psalm 119:164). Amen.

November 10

Another Advocate

"And I will ask the Father, and he will give you another Advocate, to be with you forever. This is the Spirit of truth, whom the world cannot receive, because it neither sees him nor knows him. You know him, because he abides with you, and he will be in you."

JOHN 14:16–17

When we are puzzled in life, we consult wiser, more experienced people—counselors, advocates. Their sympathetic insight clarifies and encourages. The Holy Spirit is God-living-in-us to do just such work.

What has the Counselor clarified for you?

God, why am I running to the so-called wise men of this world every time I have a problem, when you have provided me with a resident Advocate, even your Holy Spirit? I ought to be consulting you; I will consult you! In Jesus's name. Amen.

November 11

Orphaned

"I will not leave you orphaned; I am coming to you.

JOHN 14:18–19

In a little while the world will no longer see me, but you will see me; because I live, you also will live."

The desolate separation between human beings and God is overcome by Jesus. He bridges the chasm between our sin and the Father's holiness. The result is a new shared life between Creator and creature, animated by love.

How does God keep his promise?

How faithfully you keep your promises, God! Your presence drives out loneliness, your love banishes emptiness, your commands cure my aimlessness. Thank you for continuing to be with me in Jesus, through the Holy Spirit. Amen.

November 12

In

"On that day you will know that I am in my Father, and you in me, and I in you. They who have my commandments and keep them are those who love me; and those who love me will be loved by my Father, and I will love them and reveal myself to them."

John 14:20–21

"In" is the preposition of intimacy and one of the most important words in the gospel. It is later picked up by Paul and used in his famous formula "in Christ." Jesus sets us in a relationship of intimacy with himself by which we experience the fullness of God.

Read Ephesians 2:13.

Jesus, I know that you will not leave me empty or orphaned. I thank you for the promise of your presence. Invade, invigorate, inspire by your Spirit. Amen.

November 13

Those Who Love Me

Judas (not Iscariot) said to him, "Lord, how is it that you will reveal yourself to us, and not to the world?" Jesus answered him, "Those who love me will keep my word, and my Father will love them, and we will come to them and make our home with them. Whoever does not love me does not keep my words; and the word that you hear is not mine, but is from the Father who sent me."

JOHN 14:22–24

Judas's question tries to understand why God treats Christians differently from others. Jesus's answer is that he doesn't. The difference is in the love that responds to God's words and creates hospitable conditions for God's dwelling in us—"my heart Christ's home."

How does love change your relation with God?

God, I have such shallow, Hollywoodish ideas of love. I keep thinking it has to do with sunsets and soft music. You have something different in mind—not a feeling about you, but a decision for you, a decision that produces obedience and accepts your presence in Jesus Christ. Teach me such a love, for Jesus's sake. Amen.

Will Teach You Everything

"I have said these things to you while I am still with you. But the Advocate, the Holy Spirit, whom the Father will send in my name, will teach you everything, and remind you of all that I have said to you."

JOHN 14:25–26

When someone leaves us, we are poorer for their absence; when Jesus left his disciples, they were suddenly richer. They had, instead of the physical form of Jesus with them, the Holy Spirit in them.

What has the Holy Spirit taught you?

Holy Spirit, bring to my remembrance the words of Jesus that I may not be without guidance as I follow him, nor without knowledge as I speak of him, nor without peace as I trust in him. Amen.

November 15

Peace I Leave with You

"Peace I leave with you; my peace I give to you. I do not give to you as the world gives. Do not let your hearts be troubled, and do not let them be afraid."

JOHN 14:27

The world's way to get peace is to eliminate that which disturbs; God's way is to restore the unruly. The world's way to get peace is to say, "Shut up, I don't want to hear it anymore"; the Lord's way is to say, "Be still, and know that I am God." The world's peace is a precarious house of cards; God's peace is a cosmic wholeness.

How would you define peace?

"Thy mighty name salvation is, and keeps my happy soul above: comfort it brings, and power, and peace, and joy, and everlasting love: to me, with Thy great name, are given pardon and holiness and heaven." * Amen.

---

* Charles Wesley; "Thou Hidden Source of Calm Repose," *The Hymnbook*, 356.

November 16

I Am Going to the Father

"You heard me say to you, 'I am going away, and I am coming to you.' If you loved me, you would rejoice that I am going to the Father, because the Father is greater than I. And now I have told you this before it occurs, so that when it does occur, you may believe."

JOHN 14:28–29

The disciples' love for Jesus was already strong. Jesus now leads them to extend that love to the Father. As Jesus goes to the Father, he leads them (and us) through their devotion to the Father also.

Why does Jesus go away?

Father in heaven, I rejoice in these words of your son. They encourage and hearten me. Believing in him I also want to follow him until I finally arrive where he leads me—in your presence. Amen.

November 17

Let Us Be on Our Way

"I will no longer talk much with you, for the ruler of this world is coming. He has no power over me; but I do as the Father has commanded me, so that the world may know that I love the Father. Rise, let us be on our way."

John 14:30–31

Jesus had many things to say to his friends; he also had many things to show them: Jesus's words were completed in his actions. The leisurely hours of discourse led into strenuous hours of trial and crucifixion.

Are you as ready to go as to talk?

Jesus Christ: I like the way in which all your words become acts of faith and obedience. I like to ponder your words; I also like participating in your passion. Thank you for both the truths that give meaning and the commands that shape purpose in my life with you. Amen.

November 18

I Am the True Vine

"I am the true vine, and my Father is the vinegrower. He removes every branch in me that bears no fruit. Every branch that bears fruit he prunes to make it bear more fruit. You have already been cleansed by the word that I have spoken to you."

JOHN 15:1–3

Jesus is not a decorative shrub, useful for giving an aesthetic religious touch to life. He is not available to be arranged in a bouquet to delight us. He is life itself, its very center—the vine.

Compare this with Isaiah 5:1–7.

God, my habit is to think of myself as the vine with others branching off of me. How wrong! Jesus is the vine and I am a branch on him: do whatever needs to be done, Father, to make this vine-branch connection vigorous and healthy, in Jesus's name. Amen.

November 19

Abide in Me

"Abide in me as I abide in you. Just as the branch cannot bear fruit by itself unless it abides in the vine, neither can you unless you abide in me."

JOHN 15:4

It is hopeless to try to be a human being apart from Christ—just as it is impossible for a branch severed from its vine to bear grapes. The basic choice we all make is whether we will get it on our own, or "abide" in Christ, the vine.

How do you abide in Christ?

Lord, your invitation is insistently gracious. It is quite plain that you don't leave any middle ground for casual, occasional more-or-less religious visits between us. It is either "abide" or be "cast forth." I choose to abide in you, even as you have invited and commanded. Amen.

Much Fruit

"I am the vine, you are the branches. Those who abide in me and I in them bear much fruit, because apart from me you can do nothing. Whoever does not abide in me is thrown away like a branch and withers; such branches are gathered, thrown into the fire, and burned. If you abide in me, and my words abide in you, ask for whatever you wish, and it will be done for you. My Father is glorified by this, that you bear much fruit and become my disciples."

JOHN 15:5–8

The invitation to "ask whatever you will" is linked to the goal "bear much fruit." When we abide in Christ, our prayers cease to be disguised efforts to increase personal possessions and power, and become the means of being increased in Christ.

What "fruit" is promised?

Lord, I want to be so saturated with your words that when I pray the words will reappear in the midst of my asking, intermingling your will with mine, and so glorify the Father. In Jesus's name. Amen.

Abide

"As the Father has loved me, so I have loved you; abide in my love. If you keep my commandments, you will abide in my love, just as I have kept my Father's commandments and abide in his love."

JOHN 15:9–10

Christ sticks with us, through thick and thin: there is an element of perseverance to what he does, and there is also an element of serenity. Because Christ has done it, we can do it. He provides example, motive, and energy for us to live in his ways.

How many times is "abide" used?

You, O God, are steady and firm, but I am easily shaken and recurrently restless: establish me in your love, fix in me your purposes, so that I may without wavering live to your praise and glory. Amen.

November 22

My Joy ... Your Joy

"I have said these things to you so that my joy may be in you, and that your joy may be complete."

John 15:11

"Come, we that love the Lord, and let your joys be known; join in a song with sweet accord, and thus surround the throne. Let those refuse to sing who never knew our God; but children of the heavenly King should speak their joys abroad."*

What makes you joyful?

You, O God, have introduced a new kind of joy into my life—a delight in knowing that the king of creation is making something eternal in me. "Sing aloud to God our strength, shout for joy to the God of Jacob!" (Psalm 81:1). Amen.

---

* Isaac Watts, "Come, We That Love the Lord," *The Hymnbook,* 344.

November 23

Greater Love

"This is my commandment, that you love one another as I have loved you. No one has greater love than this, to lay down one's life for one's friends."

JOHN 15:12–13

If we get our ideas of love from journalists and entertainers, we will become hopelessly muddled. If we get them from Jesus Christ, we will have a clear and convincing pattern to follow as we obey his command to love one another.

How did Jesus demonstrate his love?

I don't know what more I need, Lord: you have both told me what you want me to do and showed me how to do it. In love you have given your life for me; now I give myself to you. Amen.

Friends

"You are my friends if you do what I command you. I do not call you servants any longer, because the servant does not know what the master is doing; but I have called you friends, because I have made known to you everything that I have heard from my Father."

JOHN 15:14–15

God does not turn us into robot servants so that we can help do the chores and run the errands of salvation; we become intimate friends and share the secrets of redemption.

How do friends differ from servants?

Thank you, Lord Jesus, for lifting me to where you are, for telling me your whole mind, for sharing yourself completely with me, for trusting me with your ministry, and giving me your love. Amen.

I Chose You

"You did not choose me but I chose you. And I appointed you to go and bear fruit, fruit that will last, so that the Father will give you whatever you ask him in my name. I am giving you these commands so that you may love one another."

JOHN 15:16–17

Before we ever thought of God, he thought of us. Before we decided we needed God, he decided he wanted us. He has far better plans for us than any we can think up for ourselves.

Why did God choose you?

Dear God, I know you didn't choose me without having, also, some purpose for me. Show me what you have in mind—the tasks, the blessings, the acts of love that you have for me, in Jesus's name. Amen.

November 26

You Do Not Belong to the World

"If the world hates you, be aware that it hated me before it hated you. If you belonged to the world, the world would love you as its own. Because you do not belong to the world, but I have chosen you out of the world-therefore the world hates you. Remember the word that I said to you, 'Servants are not greater than their master.' If they persecuted me, they will persecute you; if they kept my word, they will keep yours also. But they will do all these things to you on account of my name, because they do not know him who sent me."

JOHN 15:18–21

Jesus teaches us to expect neither popularity nor applause when we serve him. Christians get support not from the world, but from knowing that we are chosen by Christ for difficult service.

How do you experience the world? Rejection?

God, you know how much I want everybody to like me. Especially when I do what is good, I want them to cheer me on. But that's childish; they didn't applaud Jesus, why should they do it for me as I follow him? What I need is not the world's approval, but your blessing. Amen.

November 27

Hated

"If I had not come and spoken to them, they would not have sin; but now they have no excuse for their sin. Whoever hates me hates my Father also. If I had not done among them the works that no one else did, they would not have sin. But now they have seen and hated both me and my Father. It was to fulfill the word that is written in their law, 'They hated me without a cause.'"

JOHN 15:22–25

Why do some, when confronted with the best, choose the worst? Why do people reject God in Christ? For the person who wants to do things his or her own way, who wants to live in unrestricted selfishness and unlimited pride, Jesus is bad news.

What scripture does Jesus quote?

Lord, what you put up with from me! You patiently wait through my rebellion, my hate, my rejection—until all the energies of my sin are spent, and then receive me in love, graciously and lovingly. Thank you. Amen.

November 28

Testify

"When the Advocate comes, whom I will send to you from the Father, the Spirit of truth who comes from the Father, he will testify on my behalf. You also are to testify because you have been with me from the beginning."

JOHN 15:26–27

One way to respond to Christ is to hate him, rejecting him because he exposes our sin. Another way is to be a witness, talking to others about him in appreciation because he redeems us from our sin.

What witness do you make?

Gracious God, thank you for using me just as I am, for not waiting until I'm an expert Christian before you let me witness to your presence and lordship in my life. Keep me in readiness for the word and act that will direct another to you, through Jesus. Amen.

Keep You from Stumbling

"I have said these things to you to keep you from stumbling. They will put you out of the synagogues. Indeed, an hour is coming when those who kill you will think that by doing so they are offering worship to God. And they will do this because they have not known the Father or me. But I have said these things to you so that when their hour comes you may remember that I told you about them. I did not say these things to you from the beginning, because I was with you."

JOHN 16:1–4

Words can deceive or reveal. Words either unsettle us or assure us. The words of Jesus reveal and assure. They purge us of the greasy sediments of men's words and keep us from being poisoned by the lies of the world.

What words of Jesus do you remember best?

I'm not a steady person, God. I waver and slip. Use the words of your Son to rivet my will to you in loyal obedience that I may never fall away. I pray in Jesus's name. Amen.

November 30

Nevertheless

"But now I am going to him who sent me; yet none of you asks me, 'Where are you going?' But because I have said these things to you, sorrow has filled your hearts. Nevertheless I tell you the truth: it is to your advantage that I go away, for if I do not go away, the Advocate will not come to you; but if I go, I will send him to you."

JOHN 16:5–7

"Nevertheless" is an important gospel word: it is a pivot from the way things appear to the way things are, in Christ. It is a transition from our partial understanding to the Spirit's complete revelation.

What advantage does Jesus promise?

Lord, I get so caught up in my own plans—my childish fancies and private disappointments—that I fail to see the grand design you are working out. And then, by your grace, I see it again—a design that makes my life far richer than what I planned, more joyful than what I anticipated. Hallelujah! Amen.

December 1

Prove the World Wrong

"And when he comes, he will prove the world wrong about sin and righteousness and judgment: about sin, because they do not believe in me; about righteousness, because I am going to the Father and you will see me no longer; about judgment, because the ruler of this world has been condemned."

JOHN 16:8–11

When Jesus left his disciples, he filled the gap of his absence with a new and better presence. The Holy Spirit (the "counselor") was given to bring God's will to personal attention in regard to sin, righteousness, and judgment, three fund*Amen*tal but easily overlooked realities in our lives.

What else does the Holy Spirit do?

Holy Spirit, I open myself to your presence so you can do your work: show me my sin, create in me your righteousness, prepare me for judgment, through Jesus Christ. Amen.

December 2

Spirit of Truth

"I still have many things to say to you, but you cannot bear them now. When the Spirit of truth comes, he will guide you into all the truth; for he will not speak on his own, but will speak whatever he hears, and he will declare to you the things that are to come."

JOHN 16:12–13

Another work of the Holy Spirit (in addition to "counselor") is truth-telling. The "father of lies" has formidable opposition as the Holy Spirit keeps the word of God alive in the consciousness of each new generation.

What truth has the Holy Spirit brought home to you?

Grant, O Holy Spirit, that I may be quick to know the difference between truth and error, and then recognizing the truth, to speedily act upon it for Jesus's sake. Amen.

December 3

Declare It to You

"He will glorify me, because he will take what is mine and declare it to you. All that the Father has is mine. For this reason I said that he will take what is mine and declare it to you."

John 16:14–15

The work of the Spirit is always practical: that which is in the Father and is revealed by the Son is applied by the Spirit. As the Spirit declares to us the revelation of the Father through the Son, we are confronted and brought to faith.

What does the Spirit declare to you today?

Without your Spirit, Lord, I would procrastinate endlessly. By your Spirit I am brought to daily decisions to live by your truth and to grow in your grace. Help me to respond truly, in faith. Amen.

December 4

Your Pain Will Turn into Joy

"A little while, and you will no longer see me, and again a little while, and you will see me." Then some of his disciples said to one another, "What does he mean by saying to us, 'A little while, and you will no longer see me, and again a little while, and you will see me'; and 'Because I am going to the Father'?" They said, "What does he mean by this 'a little while'? We do not know what he is talking about." Jesus knew that they wanted to ask him, so he said to them, "Are you discussing among yourselves what I meant when I said, 'A little while, and you will no longer see me, and again a little while, and you will see me'? Very truly, I tell you, you will weep and mourn, but the world will rejoice; you will have pain, but your pain will turn into joy."

JOHN 16:16–20

The disciples had faced difficult times ahead. They were going to feel abandoned and desperate, betrayed and helpless. But their feelings, while authentic enough, would not be the reality. The reality was with God. They would learn not to interpret God's word by their feelings but let their feelings be interpreted (and changed) by God's word.

What did Jesus mean by "a little while"?

Make the word of my Lord far more real to me, O Holy Spirit, than my feelings about those words. My feelings are fickle, up one day and down the next—God's word is certain, steady, and true. Amen.

December 5

Pain

"When a woman is in labor, she has pain, because her hour has come. But when her child is born, she no longer remembers the anguish because of the joy of having brought a human being into the world. So you have pain now; but I will see you again, and your hearts will rejoice, and no one will take your joy from you."

JOHN 16:21–22

No mature woman avoids childbirth because it is painful: the joy is worth the pain. Neither do mature Christians shun discipleship because it is arduous: all the pains have a purpose and the outcome is eternally joyous.

What pains of faith are you temporarily feeling?

God, I don't want to go through my life always looking for easy, painless paths. I want to find the true way, and the straight path. I know you will give me strength to accept whatever difficulties I meet and bring me to a full life of joyous fellowship with you. Amen.

December 6

That Your Joy May Be Complete

"On that day you will ask nothing of me. Very truly, I tell you, if you ask anything of the Father in my name, he will give it to you. Until now you have not asked for anything in my name. Ask and you will receive, so that your joy may be complete."

JOHN 16:23–24

Jesus directs our faith through suffering, persecution, and pain to the completion of joy. He wants us to set our goals on the highest kind of joy and shape our prayers around that. The resurrection shows us how joy is fulfilled.

What joy has God given you?

When I encounter difficulties, Lord, help me not to be blocked by them, but rather to see through them to the joy that is prepared for me. Seeking your Easter strength, help me to find your resurrection grace adequate to my need. Amen.

December 7

_____

The Father

"I have said these things to you in figures of speech. The hour is coming when I will no longer speak to you in figures, but will tell you plainly of the Father."

JOHN 16:25

In Jesus's day most people believed there was a God, but few thought of him kindly. For those who grudgingly respected him as a far-off lawgiver, or timorously feared him as an angry judge, Jesus proclaimed him as Father and demonstrated a personal relationship with him in love.

How does the word "father" change your ideas of God?

"Our Father, who art in heaven; hallowed be thy name. Thy kingdom come, Thy will be done; on earth as it is in heaven. Give us this day our daily bread. And forgive us our sins; as we forgive those who sin against us. And lead us not into temptation; but deliver us from evil; for thine is the kingdom, and the power, and the glory, for ever. Amen."

December 8

Ask in My Name

"On that day you will ask in my name. I do not say to you that I will ask the Father on your behalf; for the Father himself loves you, because you have loved me and have believed that I came from God. I came from the Father and have come into the world; again, I am leaving the world and am going to the Father."

JOHN 16:26–28

Asking "in the name" defines our expectations in terms of God's love as revealed in Jesus. It is not a way of getting everything we want—a kind of license for indulging in fantasy and greed—but a means of receiving what God wills for us.

What will you ask from God now?

Father in heaven, I want many things; but need very few. Show me "the one thing needful" so that I may ask and receive, lacking nothing of what you will for me in Jesus. Amen.

December 9

Take Courage

His disciples said, "Yes, now you are speaking plainly, not in any figure of speech! Now we know that you know all things, and do not need to have anyone question you; by this we believe that you came from God." Jesus answered them, "Do you now believe? The hour is coming, indeed it has come, when you will be scattered, each one to his home, and you will leave me alone. Yet I am not alone because the Father is with me. I have said this to you, so that in me you may have peace. In the world you face persecution. But take courage; I have conquered the world!"

JOHN 16:29–33

Jesus "sees through" the sudden enthusiasm of the disciples. He knows that they will falter and defect in the hours just ahead. But he doesn't bawl them out; he anticipates their despair and promises his help to bring a cheerful victory in their lives.

What is the basis for the cheerful future?

You know, God, how quickly I can move from bold enthusiasm to cowering despair. Bring me through my episodes of unfaithfulness so that I may be counted among those who overcome through Jesus Christ my Lord. Amen.

December 10

Glorify Your Son

After Jesus had spoken these words, he looked up to heaven and said, "Father, the hour has come; glorify your Son so that the Son may glorify you, since you have given him authority over all people, to give eternal life to all whom you have given him. And this is eternal life, that they may know you, the only true God, and Jesus Christ whom you have sent. I glorified you on earth by finishing the work that you gave me to do. So now, Father, glorify me in your own presence with the glory that I had in your presence before the world existed."

JOHN 17:1–5

Jesus concludes his conversation with his disciples and begins to talk to God: he prays. This prayer (all of chapter 17) shows what Jesus cares about most: he traces his relationship with the Father and his intentions for people.

What is Jesus's relationship with God?

Father, thank you for letting me overhear this prayer of Jesus. It shows me what prayer can be when it matures. As I pray, bring to birth in my heart the things that really count in your eyes; in Jesus's name. Amen.

December 11

Those Whom You Gave Me

"I have made your name known to those whom you gave me from the world. They were yours, and you gave them to me, and they have kept your word. Now they know that everything you have given me is from you; for the words that you gave to me I have given to them, and they have received them and know in truth that I came from you; and they have believed that you sent me."

JOHN 17:6–8

Jesus's prayer demonstrates what von Hugel called the "deep, great fact of intercessory Prayer: that souls—all human souls— are deeply interconnected." Eternal relationships are nurtured in the exchanges between Father, Son, and men and women "whom thou gavest me."

Who prays for you?

Lord Jesus, keep me faithful in my prayers for those you have given to me: for family and friends, for neighbors and colleagues. Let my work in prayer sustain them in their work of love. Amen.

December 12

Asking on Their Behalf

I am asking on their behalf; I am not asking on behalf of the world, but on behalf of those whom you gave me, because they are yours. All mine are yours, and yours are mine; and I have been glorified in them. And now I am no longer in the world, but they are in the world, and I am coming to you. Holy Father, protect them in your name that you have given me, so that they may be one, as we are one."

JOHN 17:9–11

Jesus's ministry with us is not finished when he speaks God's word and demonstrates God's presence. He continues to guide and shape our lives by his prayers of intercession on our behalf.

How do Jesus's prayers affect you?

What a difference it makes as I pray, Father, to know that Jesus is praying for me; that my prayers to you are surrounded by his prayers for me. That makes me want to pray more than ever in the name of Jesus. Amen.

December 13

Sanctified in Truth

"While I was with them, I protected them in your name that you have given me. I guarded them, and not one of them was lost except the one destined to be lost, so that the scripture might be fulfilled. But now I am coming to you, and I speak these things in the world so that they may have my joy made complete in themselves. I have given them your word, and the world has hated them because they do not belong to the world, just as I do not belong to the world. I am not asking you to take them out of the world, but I ask you to protect them from the evil one. They do not belong to the world, just as I do not belong to the world. Sanctify them in the truth; your word is truth. As you have sent me into the world, so I have sent them into the world. And for their sakes I sanctify myself, so that they also may be sanctified in truth."

John 17:12–19

Jesus's concern for us, expressed in his prayer to the Father, is that we be set apart ("sanctified") to be examples of God's truth in the world: each Christian an instance of something that God is doing in redeeming love.

What are you set apart for?

Dear Jesus, I see what you want me to become, but I have no power in myself to produce it. I depend wholly on you to bring about the consecration you desire. Continue your prayers for me, O Christ. Amen.

December 14

That They May Be One

"I ask not only on behalf of these, but also on behalf of those who will believe in me through their word, that they may all be one. As you, Father, are in me and I am in you, may they also be in us, so that the world may believe that you have sent me. The glory that you have given me I have given them, so that they may be one, as we are one. I in them and you in me, that they may become completely one, so that the world may know that you have sent me and have loved them even as you have loved me."

JOHN 17:20–23

Jesus expands his concern: not only does he care about us as individuals, he wants us to be pleasing to God as a church so that the fellowship between the Son and the Father may be reflected in harmonious intimacy among Christians in the Church.

What separates you from other Christians?

Lord, when I hear you praying as ardently for my unity with the other people you love as you do for my unity with you, I am jarred loose from my private piety. Fulfill your prayers for my oneness with others. Amen.

Before the Foundation of the World

"Father, I desire that those also, whom you have given me, may be with me where I am, to see my glory, which you have given me because you loved me before the foundation of the world. Righteous Father, the world does not know you, but I know you; and these know that you have sent me."

JOHN 17:24–25

The ministry of Jesus is not a hastily thought-up rescue operation, instigated by God when he saw everything was going to pieces. Jesus is the consummation of an original plan for our salvation, which was set in motion "before the foundation of the world."

Compare this with Colossians 1:15–20.

My part, O God, is not to second-guess you, or offer spur-of-the-moment advice to you on how to run your world. My part is to listen and accept your love, and walk in the glorious way that you have so elaborately planned for me in Jesus. Amen.

I in Them

"I made your name known to them, and I will make it known, so that the love with which you have loved me may be in them, and I in them."

John 17:26

A brilliant conclusion to a passionate prayer: Jesus's will for us is that we be filled with the love of God, even as he himself experienced that love. Jesus, living in us, will provide both the content and the motive for the experience.

What happens as Christ lives in you?

Lord Jesus Christ, you are the great intercessor through whom all the riches of God become available to me. Live ardently in me. Thank you for your generous love and interceding grace. Amen.

December 17

Across the Kidron

He went out with his disciples across the Kidron valley to a place where there was a garden. . . . So Judas brought a detachment of soldiers together with police from the chief priests and the Pharisees, and they came there with lanterns and torches and weapons. Then Jesus, knowing all that was to happen to him, came forward and asked them, "Whom are you looking for?" They answered, "Jesus of Nazareth." Jesus replied, "I am he." Judas, who betrayed him, was standing with them. When Jesus said to them, "I am he," they stepped back and fell to the ground. Again he asked them, "Whom are you looking for?" And they said, "Jesus of Nazareth." Jesus answered, "I told you that I am he. So if you are looking for me, let these men go."

JOHN 18:1–8

The garden, long a place of quiet prayer for Jesus, now is a place of strenuous temptation. Will he accept the Father's will? Will he submit to violence by those he came to save? He will and he does. Adam's disobedience (also in a garden!) is reversed in Jesus's act of obedience and old sin becomes new righteousness.

Where is the Kidron?

I will never know, Lord Jesus, the powerful inner struggles that you endured that night; I do know that faithful prayer and a long obedience were the foundations for your victory. Use my place "across the Kidron" to prepare me for the testing and fit me for the final obedience. Amen.

December 18

Openly

So the soldiers, their officer, and the Jewish police arrested Jesus and bound him. First they took him to Annas, who was the father-in-law of Caiaphas, the high priest that year. Caiaphas was the one who had advised the Jews that it was better to have one person die for the people. Simon Peter and another disciple followed Jesus. Since that disciple was known to the high priest, he went with Jesus into the courtyard of the high priest, but Peter was standing outside at the gate. So the other disciple, who was known to the high priest, went out, spoke to the woman who guarded the gate, and brought Peter in. The woman said to Peter, "You are not also one of this man's disciples, are you?" He said, "I am not." Now the slaves and the police had made a charcoal fire because it was cold, and they were standing around it and warming themselves. Peter also was standing with them and warming himself. Then the high priest questioned Jesus about his disciples and about his teaching. Jesus answered, "I have spoken openly to the world; I have always taught in synagogues and in the temple, where all the Jews come together. I have said nothing in secret. Why do you ask me? Ask those who heard what I said to them; they know what I said." When he had said this, one of the police standing nearby struck Jesus on the face, saying, "Is that how you answer the high priest?" Jesus answered, "If I have spoken wrongly, testify to the wrong. But if I have spoken rightly, why do you strike me?" Then Annas sent him bound to Caiaphas the high priest.

JOHN 18:12–24

It is characteristic for God to act openly and publicly. Righteousness is out in the open. Goodness takes place in a light-filled creation. It is evil that is furtively plotted behind closed doors and whispered in shadows. One strong shaft of sunlight exposes its tawdry unreality.

What was the purpose of Annas's questions?

God, help me to see and respond to what is obvious: the glories of your creation and the clarities of your revelation. I will avoid all evasive mystification and walk in the open, when Jesus. Amen.

Barabbas

Now Simon Peter was standing and warming himself. They asked him, "You are not also one of his disciples, are you?" He denied it and said, "I am not." One of the slaves of the high priest, a relative of the man whose ear Peter had cut off, asked, "Did I not see you in the garden with him?" Again Peter denied it, and at that moment the cock crowed. Then they took Jesus from Caiaphas to Pilate's head-quarters. It was early in the morning. They themselves did not enter the headquarters, so as to avoid ritual defilement and to be able to eat the Passover. So Pilate went out to them and said, "What accusation do you bring against this man?" They answered, "If this man were not a criminal, we would not have handed him over to you." Pilate said to them, "Take him yourselves and judge him according to your law." The Jews replied, "We are not permitted to put anyone to death." (This was to fulfill what Jesus had said when he indicated the kind of death he was to die.) Then Pilate entered the headquarters again, summoned Jesus, and asked him, "Are you the King of the Jews?" Jesus answered, "Do you ask this on your own, or did others tell you about me?" Pilate replied, "I am not a Jew, am I? Your own nation and the chief priests have handed you over to me. What have you done?" Jesus answered, "My kingdom is not from this world. If my kingdom were from this world, my followers would be fighting to keep me from being handed over to the Jews. But as it is, my kingdom is not from here." Pilate asked him, "So you are a king?" Jesus answered, "You say that I am a king. For this I was born, and for this I came into the world, to testify to the truth. Everyone who belongs to the truth listens to my voice." Pilate asked him, "What is truth?" After he had said this, he went out to the Jews again and told them, "I find no case against him. But you have a custom that I release someone for you at the Passover. Do you want me to release for you the King of the Jews?" They shouted in reply, "Not this man, but Barabbas!" Now Barabbas was a bandit.

JOHN 18:25–40

The Substitution of Jesus for Barabbas seems like a monstrous tragedy—a preference for mediocre evil over blazing goodness. But the substitution was not fatal, for God made an act of atonement out of it whereby Barabbas also might be saved.

How do you think Barabbas felt?

Lord, I pretend indignation at the crowd's choice of Barabbas, but I do it too, choosing dull mediocrities over blazing virtues, the familiar and comfortable ways of the world over the challenging, spirit-stretching way of Christ. Forgive me and train me in better choices. Amen.

December 20

Here Is the Man!

Then Pilate took Jesus and had him flogged. And the soldiers wove a crown of thorns and put it on his head, and they dressed him in a purple robe. They kept coming up to him, saying, "Hail, King of the Jews!" and striking him on the face. Pilate went out again and said to them, "Look, I am bringing him out to you to let you know that I find no case against him." So Jesus came out, wearing the crown of thorns and the purple robe. Pilate said to them, "Here is the man!" When the chief priests and the police saw him, they shouted, "Crucify him! Crucify him!" Pilate said to them, "Take him yourselves and crucify him; I find no case against him." The Jews answered him, "We have a law, and according to that law he ought to die because he has claimed to be the Son of God."

JOHN 19:1–7

Jesus—scourged, mocked, and powerless—is still, even in the blurred vision of Pilate, the man. Just as the crowds inadvertently witnessed to Jesus's royalty, Pilate testified to his profound humanity—a complete expression of what it means to be a human being.

How are Jesus and Adam alike?

By your grace, O God, I will grow up into complete adulthood—into the measure and stature of Christ. Just as I learn the divine will from you, so I will also learn essential humanity from you, in Jesus. Amen.

December 21

Here Is Your Mother!

From then on Pilate tried to release him, but the Jews cried out, "If you release this man, you are no friend of the emperor. Everyone who claims to be a king sets himself against the emperor." When Pilate heard these words, he brought Jesus outside and sat on the judge's bench at a place called The Stone Pavement, or in Hebrew Gabbatha. Now it was the day of Preparation for the Passover; and it was about noon. He said to the Jews, "Here is your King!" They cried out, "Away with him! Away with him! Crucify him!" Pilate asked them, "Shall I crucify your King?" The chief priests answered, "We have no king but the emperor." Then he handed him over to them to be crucified. So they took Jesus; and carrying the cross by himself, he went out to what is called The Place of the Skull, which in Hebrew is called Golgotha. There they crucified him, and with him two others, one on either side, with Jesus between them. Pilate also had an inscription written and put on the cross. It read, "Jesus of Nazareth, the King of the Jews." Many of the Jews read this inscription, because the place where Jesus was crucified was near the city; and it was written in Hebrew, in Latin, and in Greek. Then the chief priests of the Jews said to Pilate, "Do not write, 'The King of the Jews,' but, 'This man said, I am King of the Jews.'" Pilate answered, "What I have written I have written." When the soldiers had crucified Jesus, they took his clothes and divided them into four parts, one for each soldier. They also took his tunic; now the tunic was seamless, woven in one piece from the top. So they said to one another, "Let us not tear it, but cast lots for it to see who will get it." This was to fulfill what the scripture says, "They divided my clothes among themselves, and for my clothing they cast lots." And that is what the soldiers did. Meanwhile, standing near the cross of Jesus were his mother, and his mother's sister, Mary the wife of Clopas, and Mary Magdalene. When Jesus saw his mother and the disciple whom he loved standing beside her, he said to his mother, "Woman, here is your son." Then he said to the disciple, "Here is your mother." And from that hour the disciple took her into his own home.

John 19:12–27

Even while doing the cosmic work of atonement, Jesus attended to domestic details: he gave his mother another son, and his disciple a new mother. The gospel creates new family ties, both of affection and responsibility, for us.

Who was the "disciple Jesus loved"?

Lord, whom do you want me to love? Whom do you want me to care for? Enlarge my sense of family beyond the walls of this house: increase my capacity for affectionate responsibility beyond this immediate family. Amen.

Finished

After this, when Jesus knew that all was now finished, he said (in order to fulfill the scripture), "I am thirsty." A jar full of sour wine was standing there. So they put a sponge full of the wine on a branch of hyssop and held it to his mouth. When Jesus had received the wine, he said, "It is finished." Then he bowed his head and gave up his spirit. Since it was the day of Preparation, the Jews did not want the bodies left on the cross during the sabbath, especially because that sabbath was a day of great solemnity. So they asked Pilate to have the legs of the crucified men broken and the bodies removed. Then the soldiers came and broke the legs of the first and of the other who had been crucified with him. But when they came to Jesus and saw that he was already dead, they did not break his legs. Instead, one of the soldiers pierced his side with a spear, and at once blood and water came out. (He who saw this has testified so that you also may believe. His testimony is true, and he knows that he tells the truth.) These things occurred so that the scripture might be fulfilled, "None of his bones shall be broken." And again another passage of scripture says, "They will look on the one whom they have pierced." After these things, Joseph of Arimathea, who was a disciple of Jesus, though a secret one because of his fear of the Jews, asked Pilate to let him take away the body of Jesus. Pilate gave him permission; so he came and removed his body. Nicodemus, who had at first come to Jesus by night, also came, bringing a mixture of myrrh and aloes, weighing about a hundred pounds. They took the body of Jesus and wrapped it with the spices in linen cloths, according to the burial custom of the Jews.

Now there was a garden in the place where he was crucified, and in the garden there was a new tomb in which no one had ever been laid. And so, because it was the Jewish day of Preparation, and the tomb was nearby, they laid Jesus there.

John 19:28–42

"Finished," used twice in these verses, has a double meaning. It means ended—the hours of agony on the cross are over and death at hand. And it means completed—the work of redemption is wholly accomplished and eternal life begun.

What scripture is quoted?

God, what you accomplished perfectly and completely in Jesus on the cross, accomplish in me. Complete and perfect that which you have begun, for Jesus's sake and by his grace. Amen.

I Have Seen the Lord

Early on the first day of the week, while it was still dark, Mary Magdalene came to the tomb and saw that the stone had been removed from the tomb. So she ran and went to Simon Peter and the other disciple, the one whom Jesus loved, and said to them, "They have taken the Lord out of the tomb, and we do not know where they have laid him." Then Peter and the other disciple set out and went toward the tomb. The two were running together, but the other disciple outran Peter and reached the tomb first. He bent down to look in and saw the linen wrappings lying there, but he did not go in. Then Simon Peter came, following him, and went into the tomb. He saw the linen wrappings lying there, and the cloth that had been on Jesus's head, not lying with the linen wrappings but rolled up in a place by itself. Then the other disciple, who reached the tomb first, also went in, and he saw and believed; for as yet they did not understand the scripture, that he must rise from the dead. Then the disciples returned to their homes. But Mary stood weeping outside the tomb. As she wept, she bent over to look into the tomb; and she saw two angels in white, sitting where the body of Jesus had been lying, one at the head and the other at the feet. They said to her, "Woman, why are you weeping?" She said to them, "They have taken away my Lord, and I do not know where they have laid him." When she had said this, she turned around and saw Jesus standing there, but she did not know that it was Jesus. Jesus said to her, "Woman, why are you weeping? Whom are you looking for?" Supposing him to be the gardener, she said to him, "Sir, if you have carried him away, tell me where you have laid him, and I will take him away." Jesus said to her, "Mary!" She turned and said to him in Hebrew, "Rabbouni!" (which means Teacher). Jesus said to her, "Do not hold on to me, because I have not yet ascended to the Father. But go to my brothers and say to them, 'I am ascending to my Father and your Father, to my God and your God.'" Mary Magdalene went and announced to the disciples, "I have seen the Lord"; and she told them that he had said these things to her.

JOHN 20:1–18

Mary is emptied of expectation and devoid of hope. Every tie to Jesus is broken and every link to Jesus severed. Out of such emptiness and loss comes the fulfillment of God's promises. "Only where graves are is resurrection" (Nietzsche).

What sorrow separates you from God?

Lord Jesus Christ, I think because you are not where I expect you that you are not anywhere; I think that because you do not appear in the way I last saw you that you are not to be seen. And you, praise God, are always surprising me with a resurrection appearance. Amen.

December 24

Peace Be with You

When it was evening on that day, the first day of the week, and the doors of the house where the disciples had met were locked for fear of the Jews, Jesus came and stood among them and said, "Peace be with you." After he said this, he showed them his hands and his side. Then the disciples rejoiced when they saw the Lord.

John 20:19–20

They supposed that the same forces that had crucified Jesus would now be directed to their destruction, and they were locked up by fear. But they were not left to such an imprisonment—Jesus released them from it with his word of peace.

Compare this with Jesus's promise in 14:27.

Too much of my life, Lord, is lived under the fearful aspect of what others think and do; stand with me and dissolve my fears, freeing me to live in your peace. Amen.

December 25

Receive the Holy Spirit

Jesus said to them again, "Peace be with you. As the Father has sent me, so I send you." When he had said this, he breathed on them and said to them, "Receive the Holy Spirit. If you forgive the sins of any, they are forgiven them; if you retain the sins of any, they are retained."

JOHN 20:21–23

The Holy Spirit is God active in us. He is not a feeling and not a sensation, but God at work in and through us. All who believe and live in the resurrection of Jesus Christ become actual participants in the risen life.

Compare this with Jesus's promise in 14:25–31.

"Breathe on me, Breath of God, until my heart is pure, until with Thee I will one will, to do and to endure. Breathe on me, Breath of God, till I am wholly Thine, until this earthly part of me glows with Thy fire divine." *
Amen.

---

* Edwin Hatch, "Breathe on Me, Breath of God," *The Hymnbook,* 206.

Do Not Doubt

But Thomas (who was called the Twin), one of the twelve, was not with them when Jesus came. So the other disciples told him, "We have seen the Lord." But he said to them, "Unless I see the mark of the nails in his hands, and put my finger in the mark of the nails and my hand in his side, I will not believe." A week later his disciples were again in the house, and Thomas was with them. Although the doors were shut, Jesus came and stood among them and said, "Peace be with you." Then he said to Thomas, "Put your finger here and see my hands. Reach out your hand and put it in my side. Do not doubt but believe." Thomas answered him, "My Lord and my God!" Jesus said to him, "Have you believed because you have seen me? Blessed are those who have not seen and yet have come to believe."

JOHN 20:24–29

Thomas is treated with great gentleness by Jesus, but yet with real firmness. His doubts are met and dealt with, but they are not made into virtues. Immaturity, while in one degree or another inevitable, is not admirable.

How are you like Thomas?

God, lead me into an Abrahamic faith that believes before it sees. Accompany me as I travel an uncertain path in the light of your certain promises and in the strong name of Jesus. Amen.

December 27

It Is the Lord!

Jesus showed himself again to the disciples by the Sea of Tiberias. . . .
Simon Peter said to them, "I am going fishing." They said to him, "We
will go with you." They went out and got into the boat, but that night
they caught nothing. Just after daybreak, Jesus stood on the beach; but
the disciples did not know that it was Jesus. Jesus said to them, "Children, you have no fish, have you?" They answered him, "No." He said
to them, "Cast the net to the right side of the boat, and you will find
some." So they cast it, and now they were not able to haul it in because
there were so many fish. That disciple whom Jesus loved said to Peter,
"It is the Lord!" When Simon Peter heard that it was the Lord, he put on
some clothes, for he was naked, and jumped into the sea. But the other
disciples came in the boat, dragging the net full of fish, for they were not
far from the land, only about a hundred yards off.

JOHN 21:1–8

The sunrise appearance of Jesus breaks in upon our lives with
explosive force. Work that was futile apart from Christ becomes
successful in his presence.

How did Peter know it was Jesus?

*Your resurrection life, Lord Jesus, is like a sunrise in work that has lost
meaning and in routines that have become pointless. Whatever my work
today, I will do it in the recognition of your presence, and under your
command. Amen.*

December 28

Full of Large Fish

When they had gone ashore, they saw a charcoal fire there, with fish on it, and bread. Jesus said to them, "Bring some of the fish that you have just caught." So Simon Peter went aboard and hauled the net ashore, full of large fish, a hundred fifty-three of them; and though there were so many, the net was not torn. Jesus said to them, "Come and have breakfast." Now none of the disciples dared to ask him, "Who are you?" because they knew it was the Lord. Jesus came and took the bread and gave it to them, and did the same with the fish. This was now the third time that Jesus appeared to the disciples after he was raised from the dead.

JOHN 21:9–14

The catch of fish demonstrated that the risen Christ was among them in their daily work, giving completion and meaning to it. The resurrection transforms Monday work as much as Sunday worship.

What resurrection appearances preceded this one?

Lord, in my unbelief I don't expect you to take an interest in my work-day routines; your appearance is a welcome surprise, commanding, transforming, sustaining. All praise to you, risen Christ. Amen.

Yes, Lord

When they had finished breakfast, Jesus said to Simon Peter, "Simon son of John, do you love me more than these?" He said to him, "Yes, Lord; you know that I love you." Jesus said to him, "Feed my lambs." A second time he said to him, "Simon son of John, do you love me?" He said to him, "Yes, Lord; you know that I love you." Jesus said to him, "Tend my sheep." He said to him the third time, "Simon son of John, do you love me?" Peter felt hurt because he said to him the third time, "Do you love me?" And he said to him, "Lord, you know everything; you know that I love you." Jesus said to him, "Feed my sheep."

JOHN 21:15–17

The patient persistence of Jesus's questions probes beneath the sin and guilt of Peter's recent denials (see John 18:15–27) and builds a new identity as Christ's disciple. The triple affirmation of love matches and overcomes the triple denial. Peter is restored.

Why is Peter singled out?

How grateful I am, Father, that you do "not deal with us according to our sins, nor requite us according to our iniquities" (Psalm 103:10) but treat us with mercy and grace. Restore me to your fellowship and make me strong in your service. Amen.

December 30

What Is That to You?

Peter turned and saw the disciple whom Jesus loved following them; he was the one who had reclined next to Jesus at the supper and had said, "Lord, who is it that is going to betray you?" When Peter saw him, he said to Jesus, "Lord, what about him?" Jesus said to him, "If it is my will that he remain until I come, what is that to you? Follow me!" So the rumor spread in the community that this disciple would not die. Yet Jesus did not say to him that he would not die, but, "If it is my will that he remain until I come, what is that to you?"

JOHN 21:20–23

It is not given to us to know what God is doing with others; we need to pay attention to what he is doing with us. Disciples are not permitted to gossip, even if the gossip is about God. It is enough to know that he says to us, Follow me!

What did Jesus mean?

Dear God, deliver me from the curiosity that asks questions about what is none of my business. Bring me back to the point of faith where I respond to you, the place of obedience where I believe in you, and the path of love where I follow you, in Jesus's name. Amen.

December 31

Also Many Other Things

This is the disciple who is testifying to these things and has written them, and we know that his testimony is true. But there are also many other things that Jesus did; if every one of them were written down, I suppose that the world itself could not contain the books that would be written.

JOHN 21:24–25

With wonderful skill and impeccable veracity, John has written what we need to know of Jesus and our salvation. He has not indulged our curiosity. He has not overloaded us with information and incident. From now on all our energy goes into belief and obedience and praise.

Do you ever find yourself wondering about the things you don't know instead of obeying the things right before you?

Lord Jesus Christ, thank you for giving me enough but not too much. Now keep me believing and obedient before this spare and inviting story. Help me to assimilate your life into my life and daily live praising your glory. Amen.